The Norwegian-American Historical Association
1925–1975

ODD S. LOVOLL

and

KENNETH O. BJORK

1975

The Norwegian-American Historical Association

NORTHFIELD • MINNESOTA

Lithographed in the United States of America at the
North Central Publishing Company, St. Paul.

PREFACE

THE executive board of the Norwegian-American Historical Association authorized the publication of this brief study of the society as part of the observance in 1975 of its half-century of activity. Copies of the review, it was decided, should be distributed to the Association's members and to other interested individuals and institutions. Dr. Odd S. Lovoll and I were commissioned to undertake the task of preparing the history.

Our original plan was to spend the major part of the summer of 1974 researching and writing the booklet. An accident in late June involving me, and my subsequent hospitalization and slow recovery, however, placed the entire task of research on the shoulders of Dr. Lovoll, who also prepared a preliminary draft of the review. During the following winter months, we jointly revised his manuscript and added to it — slightly revised — my "Plan for the Future," originally published in the July, 1974, *Swedish Pioneer Historical Quarterly*, an issue honoring Professor Franklin D. Scott.

We present the following pages in the hope that they will not only inspire pride in the work of the past fifty years, but will also strengthen the resolve of members to co-operate in realizing the dreams of the Association's founders in October, 1925.

K.O.B.

CONTENTS

INTRODUCTION

In 1938 the Norwegian-American Historical Association, then only thirteen years of age, prepared a history of its activity and plotted a long-range program for the future in a pamphlet written by Kenneth O. Bjork and Theodore C. Blegen and titled ''A Review and a Challenge.'' The Association already had established a proud record and had won respect and acclaim from an international community of scholars. It could point to nineteen publications of merit, the product of rigid scholarship, careful editing, and professional printing. The Association had engaged effectively in collecting historical documents, in promoting research, and in building a stable and enthusiastic membership.

''Challenge'' is still a timely expression as the Association reviews fifty years of service and fifty-five publications and once again makes projections into the future. In some areas the challenge has been met. The Association has found new fields to investigate, utilized a variety of source materials, attracted devoted scholars, pursued an aggressive editorial policy, enjoyed a progressive leadership, maintained a sound financial status, and retained interested members from all walks of life. Its rich program has resulted in significant studies that bring into focus the Norwegian-American experience and its relationship to that of all ethnic groups in the United States.

Yet much remains to be done if the Association is to fulfill its mission. As additional generations of Norwegian Americans appear on the historical scene, and as the need arises to interpret the past anew and from a longer perspective, the challenge accepted by a few men fifty years ago becomes ever more complex and urgent. Until the full story has been told of the peoples constituting the American nation, its history and character cannot be accurately comprehended or assessed. The many ethnic groups must themselves make known and interpret the circumstances and incidents attending their migration and existence in the New World. An understanding of American nationalism must with inevitable logic be sought in the diversity of our population and be found in a sympathetic interpretation and acceptance of individuals and peoples with varying interests and backgrounds.

I

THE NORWEGIAN AMERICANS

ORGANIZED immigration to America from Norway began with the arrival of the sloop *Restauration* in the port of New York on October 9, 1825. The landing of this tiny vessel with its fifty-three passengers and crew, after a fourteen-week voyage from Stavanger on the southwestern coast of Norway, has the appeal and fascination that accompany the beginnings of any important historical movement. The story of these pioneer immigrants — religious dissenters, some of them Quakers — has been told and retold. They had been guided by the enigmatic Cleng Peerson — "the pathfinder of Norwegian emigration" — whose biography may never be fully written.

After the coming of the "Sloopers," as the first immigrants generally are called, eleven years passed before the second shipload of Norwegians landed in the New World. Thereafter, a constant stream of people flowed to America. At times it rose to a mighty torrent. By the outbreak of the Civil War, nearly 70,000 Norwegians had entered the United States. The first great wave in the Atlantic crossing began in 1866 and continued into the mid-1870s. The second and greatest period of migration was in the 1880s, when eleven out of every thousand Norwegians were leaving the homeland annually. The movement to the New World reached a climax in 1882, when more than 28,000 left Norway. The first decade of the present century witnessed the final great exodus. When legislation in the

United States and more favorable prospects at home effectively curtailed immigration in the 1920s, no fewer than 800,000 Norwegians had made the crossing to America. With their descendants, the immigrants constitute at least three million citizens in this country, a number that approaches the present population of Norway.

The pattern of Norwegian settlement in the United States resulted from a northwestward advance. The newcomers were attracted to the prairies of the Upper Middle West, where they shared in the agricultural production of the New World. The early immigrant treasured the value and security provided by the ownership of land, and it was land he had dreamed of securing in America. As the frontier moved westward, Norwegians followed in its trek, coming either directly from the homeland or from older "colonies" to the east. The major area of settlement was in the upper Mississippi and Missouri valleys, spreading from Illinois into the states of Wisconsin, Iowa, Minnesota, and the Dakotas.

When the best land in the Middle West had been taken by the close of the century, the Norwegians went elsewhere — to Montana, Idaho, and Washington, as well as into the prairie provinces of Canada. After about 1890, an increasing proportion also settled in larger cities. Brooklyn on the eastern seaboard, Seattle on Puget Sound, and Chicago and Minneapolis in the Middle West became distinct centers of immigrant activity. In smaller numbers, they also settled outside these areas, forming ethnic pockets in Texas, California, Utah, Oregon, and Alaska. In the period from about 1895 to 1925, when the number of European-born was greatest, a "Norwegian America" flourished.

A unique immigrant culture evolved, elements of the old-country heritage mingling subtly with American influences. Out of a Lutheran state-church tradition emerged a free church, split into a number of synods with conflicting theological positions. Denominations outside the Lutheran tradition, such as the Mormons, the Methodists, and the Baptists, also won immigrant converts. Early pastors keenly felt the need to train ministers of the gospel and desired to preserve Norwegian values. Such considerations, combined with the necessity of newcomers to adjust to the American environment, resulted in the founding of numerous academies and colleges. These institutions have been imbued with an abiding faith in the salutary benefits of a Christian education.

A large foreign-language press served the Norwegian Americans. Its very size reflects the character of the immigrant society. Files of numerous newspapers remain significant sources for the study of the Norwegian-American community. Together with other printed materials, they present a vast documentation of the hopes, ambitions, and accomplishments — as well as disappointments, struggles, and failures — of a literate and highly vocal national group.

A special literature emerged, directed at the immigrants. Its foremost exponent was Ole E. Rølvaag. In a superb novel, *Giants in the Earth*, he gave expression to the tribulations and alienation of the immigrant, but also reflected his pioneer joy in conquest and his faith in the future. The novel was quickly seized upon by other Americans as a part of their own history. Many writers sought to recreate in fiction the circumstances surrounding the pioneer experience.

A language best described as Norwegian-American was used by the immigrants and passed on to their children in many settlements. Especially in the cities, a lively culture and social life prevailed. It embraced the activity of singing societies, male choruses, library, literary, and debate groups, athletic clubs, and a number of societies that spoke for a wide variety of causes and interests. Through mutual-benefit organizations, the immigrants attempted to protect themselves against economic want. In the *bygdelag*, they convened around the ordinary and the cherished in their national heritage as they knew it in their homeland districts.

Norwegian Americans entered into all phases of business, cultural, professional, and political life. They contributed to American maritime history, both on the seas and on inland waters. They plied a number of trades, and on the west coast helped to develop the fishing industry. They labored in the logging camps and prospected in the gold fields of California, the Rockies, and Alaska. Accustomed to democratic ways in Norway, they entered with ease into the political life of the country and developed a leadership from their own ranks. Strongly imbued with a sense of community, they revealed a bent for reformist policies. They became doctors, professors, lawyers, engineers, and entered into a variety of other professions. Some founded industries and became prominent men of business. In whatever manner they lived out their lives, they also left records of their activities.

With the passing of the original immigrants and the gradual loss of the Norwegian language in subsequent generations, the old-world hold weakened. Time has not, however, wholly erased a consciousness of Norwegian identity, although this has not always been attended by a feeling of great pride. Until the past few years, Norwegians have at times demonstrated little interest in their own past and instead have often evidenced resentment of things related to their tradition. Marcus L. Hansen, in his belief that the third generation would express a renewed concern, was overly optimistic. Signs at present, however, indicate that at least some Americans of Norwegian descent are re-examining their past and reconsidering its implications. This tendency is reflected in college life, in adult education, in social activities, and in visits to ancestral homes.

II

A VIEW FROM THE 1970s

THE Norwegian-American Historical Association came into being
when the era of free immigration had ended — a hundred years after
the arrival in America of the first shipload of Norwegian immigrants. Some leaders thought that the time was close at hand when
the immigrants would be completely assimilated in the American
melting pot. A champion for the retention of Norwegian language
and culture in this country, Waldemar Ager, even viewed the forma-
tion of the Association as an unfortunate sign of the times. He
compared it to the action of an old man ready to die who wants to
put his affairs in order: Norwegian Americans would no longer
make history but would only write it.

Needless to say, Ager has been proved wrong, both in his as-
sessment of Norwegian-American institutions and in the role played
by the Association. A variety of stages and external circumstances
have marked the development of the latter. The Association sur-
vived the financial strictures imposed by the depression of the 1930s,
kept faith during the period of World War II, and, with the
coming of peace, embarked upon an ambitious publication program. In general, however, the period from about 1950, with its
emphasis on consensus and the denial of social and political diversity, represented a low point in the field of immigration history.

In the next decade, the articulation of Black consciousness insti-
gated a new era in the study of American social conditions. A white

ethnic self-assertion followed upon the increase of Black pride, and a somewhat surprised academic community discovered that ethnicity was still very much in existence. The resurgence of ethnic awareness reverberated even in such terms as "Polish power," "Italian power," and "Irish power" — all reflecting the struggle for equality and liberation from the stigma of inferiority contained in the expression "Black power." The 1970s has therefore been labeled by some the decade of white ethnic pride. In this context, we must regard the evidences of renewed fascination with national and family backgrounds within the Norwegian-American group, although they have been relatively mild in character.

The over-all revival of interest in ethnicity, as well as the growth of scholarly concern for the ethnic dimension in American history, can be traced to a number of circumstances. In part, the causes may be sought in a preoccupation with diversity and individuality. The prime sources of a racial, cultural, linguistic, and religious pluralism can be found in the immigrant tradition. Ethnic interest may, in addition, be related to the so-called "nostalgia boom," a groping for a secure and firm past as an anchor in the uncertainties and fast changes in present society, and also to a rising interest in the nation's Bicentennial in 1976, when Americans will re-examine and re-evaluate the historical factors that have shaped and sustained American nationhood for two hundred years.

Immigration studies have benefited from progress made in other fields of knowledge. The growth of a respectable history of labor, with a broad concern for the worker rather than for the elite in the labor movement or for the institutions he serves, has created the term "bottom-up history." This evidence of interest in the role of the common man has led many to turn to the study of the immigrant. The social sciences have developed methods of gathering information for large numbers of people. From such data, it is possible to make far-reaching quantitative analyses. Greater precision has become possible in the study of voting patterns, mobility, and social relationships. The quantitative approach has made possible a large number of inferences from various numerical associations when these are programmed into a computer. A resurgence of interest in immigrant history has thus come about because of methodological advances.

The new techniques have often been interdisciplinary in nature. Sociology, psychology, and history have blended to produce significant studies of immigrant life in such areas as language and cultural retention and in social mobility. They have charted the ethnic impact on social, cultural, and political institutions and traditions. Increasingly, the studies have become comparative in their approach, treating several ethnic groups. An international dimension also has been added to show that migration to America was part of a larger movement. Environment is thereby seen as a variable in the life of an ethnic group.

Progress in the field of immigration history will ultimately produce a more complete delineation of the mechanics of acculturation and maintenance within the immigrant community. The study of the role of the individual family as the bearer of tradition in an ethnic group is essential to a full understanding of American life. Such an approach, soundly pluralistic, will establish the nature of identity and awareness, at times so subtle that it is hard to discern. It may require an investigation of the whole spectrum of human existence. Michael Novak, in his recent book, *The Rise of the Unmeltable Ethnics: Politics and Culture in the Seventies*, outlines the scope of the examination: "I am fascinated by instincts, emotions, images, hardly articulate ways of feeling, the movements of the stomach, habits, traditions: The organic networks of actual human life transmitted from generation to generation." The new history could thus provide a relaxed understanding and an informed appreciation of an individual's roots and of the historical and social processes that explain his particular circumstances.

The old immigration history was limited by the fact that it emerged partly out of polemics over restriction during the early decades of the present century. It was marred by the concept of "desirable" and "undesirable" immigrants. It expressed a conviction, conscious or unconscious, that the melting pot worked. Progressive historians, who first addressed themselves to immigration as a significant factor in the nation's development, viewed American history as a process of struggle and growth toward a democratic order. From such a viewpoint, ethnic diversity represented an unnatural element. The progressive concept therefore demanded a rapid and total assimilation of all foreign ingredients. Thus the many notices of the imminent demise of ethnicity, and also surprise at its continued existence and growth during the past decade.

It is not surprising that the immigrants themselves wished to make their story known before supposedly they would pass out of existence as distinct national groups. As a consequence, a "contribution" school of historians evolved that extolled the virtues and importance to America of various ethnic elements. Although their writings have been downgraded as biased and chauvinistic, it must in fairness be stated that the immigrant recorders were not the only filiopietists in our society. History of their kind is still being produced, and it serves, together with an increasing volume of genealogical listings, to kindle the fires of ethnic pride.

There also appeared, in the 1930s and 1940s, a number of historians who approached the immigrant community on its own terms, presenting a broad human interpretation of its experience. Oscar Handlin's *Boston's Immigrants: A Study in Acculturation*, published in 1941, represented a genuine break-through in historical research. It analyzed the impact of immigration upon the culture, economy, ecology, and social structure of Boston. Even before Handlin, Theodore C. Blegen, through his work in the Norwegian-American Historical Association, had lifted the study of a particular immigrant group to the highest level of scholarship. In his writings we find no special pleading, but instead sympathetic and broad interpretation of Norwegian-American life. Marcus L. Hansen, also on the editorial board of the Association, grasped the significance of the Atlantic crossing as it related to the full sweep of American history. Enduring accomplishments in the field of immigration history were also made by George M. Stephenson for the Swedes and by Carl Wittke for the Germans.

III

THE ASSOCIATION'S BACKGROUND

LONG before the creation of the Norwegian-American Historical Association, immigrant writers had entered the field of historical research. The bias and the glorification of the deeds of their forefathers expressed by these recorders have caused some scholars to dismiss their accounts as merely filiopietistic. The pioneer approach to immigration history has, however, merged in a fortunate manner with the professional integrity and critical scholarship of trained historians to bring about the founding of the Association. Deep filiopietism, a mode of ancestral worship and respect, has to the present significantly provided the organization with devoted members and led to liberal donations.

Literary productions by amateur historians and folklorists began to appear almost with the arrival of the first immigrants. Without the dedicated services of these interested individuals, the saga of the transplanted Norwegian could not have been told in its entirety. A quick scanning of the works of established historians will convince anyone of their indebtedness to the early writers. The self-centered character of the first ethnic history can be explained in terms of the lowly position occupied by the immigrant. He felt a need to protest his inferior status; frequently he was filled with indignation at the lack of understanding of his plight, and he harbored a strong desire both to identify with American society and to establish his contributions to its welfare.

The very first immigrant writers who realized the value of historical records actually displayed remarkable restraint, giving factual
and partly interpretive accounts of pioneer conditions. Claus L.
Clausen, early pastor among the immigrants and editor of *Emigranten* (The Emigrant), sent a complete volume of his newspaper for
the year 1851 to the State Historical Society of Wisconsin. He had
been motivated, as he stated in *Emigranten*, by a deep concern: "If
we do not wish . . . veils of secrecy to rest over our times and
conditions as now cover the early history of the Indians . . . we
must preserve what we can of that which is worthwhile in regard to
our conditions and relations of life." He solicited communications
about Norwegian settlements in Wisconsin, working with the historical society to have such collections listed in its annual reports.
Another early writer and promoter of immigration history was Svein
Nilsson, who edited and published *Billed-Magazin* (Picture
Magazine) from 1868 to 1870 in Madison. In this journal he printed
valuable articles on Scandinavian settlements based on personal
interviews; they were authentic and well written.

At about the same time, Rasmus Bjørn Anderson, professor in the
University of Wisconsin from 1869 to 1883, established the special
pleading and apologetics of the filiopietistic historical tradition in
his lectures on Leif Ericson, the early discoverer of the American
continent. His presentations were a far cry from the modest and
sober accounts prepared by Nilsson. Through his lectures, writings,
and newspaper enterprise, Anderson did, however, generate a lively
interest in immigrant history, and his book, *The First Chapter in
Norwegian Immigration (1821–1840): Its Causes and Results*, published in 1894, was on the whole a competent work.

A definite desire to establish a society to preserve historical records may be viewed in relationship to a strong local-history movement from the second half of the nineteenth century. The State
Historical Society of Wisconsin, founded at mid-century in Madison, developed into a model for the western type of state historical
society. Under aggressive and innovative leadership, it became the
first institution of its kind, recognizing its responsibilities in public
education and departing from the "gentlemen's club" character of
many earlier organizations. From its inception, it was involved in
collecting, editing, and publishing historical papers and documents;

with the democratic advances at the turn of the century, its broader progressive quality developed.

The Wisconsin society provided both an incentive and a model for similar endeavors. Lloyd Hustvedt, in a recent article on the antecedents of the Association, credits the Reverend Samson Madsen Krogness with being the first individual to speak for the establishment of a historical organization among the Norwegian immigrants. He had a large library of Norwegian-American materials, and in 1884 he outlined in a letter to John A. Johnson, an industrialist in Madison, Wisconsin, complete plans for such a society — replete with a central committee, state-level divisions, and an arrangement for funding through membership dues. In 1898, after a period of published historical accounts by Knud Langeland, editor of *Skandinaven* (Chicago), Johannes B. Wist of *Decorah-Posten*, and Rasmus Bjørn Anderson, the idea of organizing a historical society was again introduced by Professor Nils Flaten of St. Olaf College in a letter to Professor O. G. Felland, librarian at the same institution. Nothing, however, came of these early efforts.

Further progress derived from lively Norwegian-American organizational drives after the turn of the century. High hopes were placed in the *bygdelag* — societies of immigrants from a particular valley, settlement, or district in the old country. The deep consciousness of regional origins in the immigrant body eventually produced close to half a hundred *bygdelag*, the majority organizing before World War I. To their primary social functions, centering about annual summer reunions, they added the collection of historical and biographical data about their own folk.

In 1909, when representatives from several of the *bygdelag* convened in Minneapolis to plan for a joint *lag* celebration commemorating the centennial of Norwegian independence in 1914, they determined to co-ordinate efforts in other areas as well. The various societies had already published yearbooks and periodicals containing valuable reminiscent and historical material. They were aware of the urgency of preserving their history for posterity. Out of such considerations grew the idea of beginning archives, a museum, and even a historical society, all to be located on the campus of the University of Minnesota in Minneapolis. After 1912, a *bygdelag* committee seriously considered the feasibility of such a center.

Unfortunately, conflicting interests within the Norwegian-American community, especially concerning the location of the source collections, killed the grandly envisioned plan. The major champions of the center were D. G. Ristad and Andrew A Veblen, president of Valdres Samband, the first *bygdelag* organized in 1902. In 1930, Veblen wrote to O. E. Rølvaag, then secretary for the Norwegian-American Historical Association: "I have at times felt a wistful regret, because I failed to possess your confidence to the extent that we might have co-operated in 1914. Possibly thus the Historical Association might have dated from that year."

Det Norske Selskap (The Norwegian Society), founded in 1903, at one time tried unsuccessfully to form an umbrella over the *bygdelag* in an effort to guide their collecting of historical information. Its interests were, however, mainly literary, although it did support the writings of Hjalmar Rued Holand, farmer-historian in Wisconsin. George T. Flom, an established scholar in the University of Illinois, in 1909 published *A History of Norwegian Immigration to the United States*. Martin Ulvestad, too, collected vast amounts of information from the pioneer era.

Symra, located in Decorah, Iowa, and like the Norwegian Society chiefly a literary club, showed some promise of developing into a historical body. Its periodical *Symra*, which appeared after 1905, also addressed itself to immigrant history. From 1907 on there was discussion of making the Symra society into a historical institution, and when the group's official journal discontinued publication in 1914, Knut Gjerset, professor at Luther College, discussed with Kristian Prestgard and Johannes B. Wist, both of *Decorah-Posten*, the possibility of issuing a yearbook in English and promoting a historical society. In 1922, Gjerset took steps to carry the plan through, and in 1923 even attempted to set up an editorial board and to discuss a publication program with Augsburg Publishing House. Like the earlier efforts, it came to naught.

The grand festivities of May, 1914, in Minneapolis and St. Paul, celebrating the rebirth of Norway as a nation on May 17, 1814 — the date of the signing of its constitution — also created considerable interest in the immigrant past. The effort in preceding years to establish archives, a museum, and a historical society had been made in anticipation of the favorable surge of nationalism the occasion was expected to generate. One individual who found the time opportune for an organizational push was Thorstein Jahr of the Library of Congress in Washington, D.C. His position had given him insights into early Norwegian migration, and in the fall of 1913 he made a lecture tour through the Middle West, speaking on migration from Norway through the Netherlands in the seventeenth century. He ended his lectures with a strong appeal to found a historical society, and he agitated for the same project in the immigrant press. No such body emerged out of the jubilee spirit, however, despite great hopes, and World War I silenced further agitation for many years.

IV

THE ASSOCIATION IS ORGANIZED

THE philosophical tenets of the Norwegian-American Historical Association were directly related to the new scholarship created by Frederick Jackson Turner and Charles A. Beard. Even though these scholars differed greatly in emphasis, they both saw environment and economic forces as determining factors in history. Turner was perhaps the first to address himself to the study of immigration. In the 1890s, as professor in the University of Wisconsin, he formulated his famous frontier thesis. According to Turner, the impact of the frontier was to Americanize, liberate, and fuse the Europeans into a new and mixed nation. The professional historians who shaped the Association belonged to the Turnerian generation. Their works became a history of transition — a tale that presupposed the theme of the adaptation of old-world cultures to the new-world environment. Unlike Turner, however, they took into account the great diversity of backgrounds in the immigrant groups. They also revealed a strong sense of professionalism and dedication to their task. Edward N. Saveth has described how scholars like Marcus L. Hansen, Theodore C. Blegen, Oscar Handlin, Caroline Ware, and others of this generation combined careful documentation with tempered judgment in writing the immigrant saga. With these scholars, minority apologetics gave way to a broader and more fruitful approach.

In 1925 the time was favorable for the organization of the Association. American historiography had attained considerable maturity. Norwegian migration had run its course, and the immigrant experience could be told with authority. It is likely that few of those who took part in the Association's founding fully understood the advances that had been made in American historical scholarship. They were, on the whole, still influenced by the desire to record the merits of their ancestors in the tradition of the amateur writers of previous decades.

Again, as in 1914, a grand celebration became the focal point for organizational endeavors. A Norse-American Centennial to commemorate a century of Norwegian migration — directed mainly by the *bygdelag* and attracting a broad participation and widespread attention — was successfully concluded in Minnesota's Twin Cities from June 6 to 9, 1925. It stimulated great nationalistic pride. President Calvin Coolidge contributed to ethnic enthusiasm by his presence and remarks on this occasion.

For a second time, the spark that kindled discussion came from Washington, D.C., in the person of Carl Tellefsen, correspondent for *Decorah-Posten*, who in a communication to the paper on July 18, 1924, pleaded for a historical society, stating: "I feel that this [the Norse-American Centennial] is the psychological moment for finally organizing an institution we have missed for such a long time." Excited responses appeared editorially both in *Decorah-Posten* and in *Minneapolis Tidende* (Minneapolis Times).

Thorstein Jahr restated his earlier arguments for such a learned society in several journals. In October, 1924, an invitation for an organizational meeting during the 1925 festivities, signed by thirty-six men, appeared in the press. After encouragement from Gisle Bothne, professor in the University of Minnesota, Theodore C. Blegen prepared a constitution which he had printed in *Minneapolis Tidende*. The organizational meeting, which had been scheduled for 10:00 a.m. of June 8 on the state fair grounds, failed because of mismanagement or misunderstanding. Only Kristian Prestgard and Knut Gjerset arrived on time, and, after they had left, Blegen, who had been presenting a speech at the fair grounds grandstand, N.N. Rønning of Minneapolis, and A. O. Barton of Madison, Wisconsin, appeared. Organization therefore "came to nothing," as Prestgard complained editorially in *Decorah-Posten*.

Knut Gjerset had been responsible for a noteworthy exhibit of Norwegian-American artifacts during the Centennial. It is not surprising that he should have felt great responsibility for the preservation of such materials. He had been in charge of a museum housed on the campus of Luther College since 1922. Together with Kristian Prestgard, he called a meeting for July 24 at the latter's home, "Troldhaugen," in Decorah. A small group of men, fourteen in all counting a few interested persons who could not attend, effected an organization with the lengthy name Society for the Preservation of Historical Relics and Records of Norwegian-American Pioneer and Cultural Life. They were primarily concerned with developing the Decorah museum, and wanted to secure support for it in a future historical society. The assembled men also envisioned, however, a total cultural effort focused in three areas: a museum in Decorah, a collection of Norwegian literature and music at St. Olaf College, and a center for art in Minneapolis.

The men who gathered in Decorah contributed ten dollars each to make it possible for Gjerset, who had chaired the meeting, to travel and solicit support for their proposal. When Gjerset, accompanied by Prestgard, came to St. Olaf, he met with resolute opposition from a group headed by O. E. Rølvaag, who feared vested interests on behalf of the museum and offered support only if they could proceed with the understanding that no previous plans had been made. Rølvaag then escorted Gjerset and Prestgard on a trip to Minneapolis, St. Paul, and Eau Claire, Wisconsin, to confer with Waldemar Ager, editor of *Reform*, at the last city. A hundred potential members of a society were enrolled, and, as a result of the action of these men, a meeting was called for October 6, 1925, at St. Olaf College. As a sign of good will, the invitation was made in the name of the organization created in Decorah in July. Gjerset, Prestgard, Rølvaag, and D. G. Ristad met on October 5 to prepare for the meeting. Gjerset had the task of drawing up a constitution and by-laws. Then, on the following day, October 6, fifty-two persons adopted the constitution, elected officers, and consummated the organization.

The Norwegian-American Historical Association was duly incorporated under the laws of Minnesota on February 4, 1926. A successful effort had thus been launched, but at the time it was uncertain what could be accomplished in the future. A number of organizations had come and gone in the immigrant community without leaving any significant mark. The challenge that faced the early promoters was tremendous. The constitution envisaged an executive board with "a President, one or more Vice Presidents, a Secretary, a Treasurer, and such other officers as may be elected." The board would meet when called by the president. The election of these directors and other business were to be conducted by the general membership at triennial meetings, beginning in 1927. The executive board was to appoint a board of publications and a board of finance. Clearly, the men who built the framework were serious in their determination to develop a learned society without the added appeal of social activity.

The Association's certificate of incorporation stated in general terms that the purpose of the organization was to "engage in all activities necessary, useful, or expedient for the collection and dissemination of information about the people in the United States of Norwegian birth and descent and to preserve the same in appropriate forms as historic records." The first executive board consisted of D. G. Ristad, president; Laurence M. Larson, vice president; O. E. Rølvaag, secretary; O. M. Oleson, treasurer; Birger Osland, assistant treasurer; and A. C. Floan and Knut Gjerset. Theodore C. Blegen was to head the editorial board, assisted by Gjerset and Prestgard. The founders held great expectations as to what these men could do to promote Norwegian-American culture on a broad front.

V

THE NORWEGIAN-AMERICAN MUSEUM

THE second objective of the Association, as formulated in the original constitution, was to sponsor the Norwegian-American Historical Museum in Decorah, Iowa. It is, of course, clear that documents in the larger sense include typical museum pieces: buildings, implements, clothing, ornaments, and other artifacts. The Association therefore embraced with enthusiasm the idea of supporting the museum. This institution has operated independently, however, and has financed its own activities.

The museum originated at Luther College, which began in 1861. Its beginnings are shrouded in some obscurity, although the year assigned for its start is 1877. The idea of a museum developed out of the collection by Luther College teachers, interested in origins, of objects preserved in the homes of early settlers in America. When the main building of the college was rebuilt after a fire in 1889, a small room was set aside for artifacts, with William Sihler in charge of the modest collection. The number of museum pieces grew as a result of appeals made to alumni and friends.

In 1895, Luther College Museum, as it was then called, was moved to a nearby brick structure, and Haldor Hanson was assigned to look after the few objects in its possession. Hanson became a tireless promoter of the museum idea — both to increase the collection and to secure better facilities for it. He was the first person to hold the title of curator. When he left in 1902, he had been able to arouse considerable interest and enthusiasm for the project. He gave the museum direction — that of gathering all that threw light on the contributions to this country by persons of Norwegian descent. It has never lost sight of this objective.

During the following years, Geroge Markhus, H. W. Sheel, M. K. Bleken, and C. K. Preus, president of Luther, occupied the curatorship. Then, in 1922, Knut Gjerset became curator of the museum's limited and partly disorganized collection. In a short time, he made great progress in developing a collection of value and one that gained respect. He expanded the museum's space and arranged a number of informative exhibits. Gjerset was a large-visioned scholar, who made it possible for later generations to visualize the living conditions of their pioneer ancestors in America. He dreamed of a merger of the museum and the projected historical society. An excellent start was made at the time of the organization of the Norwegian-American Historical Association, and developments in 1926 gave promise of continued unity. That year a committee in Norway informed the Association through Anders Sandvig, director of the Maihaugen Museum at Lillehammer, that a collection of artifacts was being given to the Norwegians in America. The Association accepted the generous gift and determined that the articles should be deposited at Decorah, with the Norwegian-American Historical Museum — from October 15, 1925, its official name — as permanent custodian. The collection included hundreds of extremely valuable items from museums in Norway. These greatly stimulated the collection of artifacts in this country.

Important acquisitions were made for both the indoor exhibits and for the outdoor museum that had grown up on the campus of the college. They include typical dwellings furnished with pieces brought from Norway or made by the immigrants on the frontier, and log cabins that were moved to Decorah from their original sites. The Erik Egge cabin, built in 1851–1852, housed the Reverend and Mrs. U. V. Koren in 1853–1854 and is termed the first Lutheran parsonage west of the Mississippi; Little Iowa cabin, built by Hans Haugen in Winneshiek County, Iowa, was once used as a parochial schoolhouse. The millstones of the Old Mill were brought from

Valdres, Norway, by Knut Gudmundson Norsving in 1849 and were used for grinding grain and malt. A little log house, used for drying grain and malt, came from Goodhue County, Minnesota. The museum houses the Slooper Collection, which consists of relics presented by the Slooper Society, weapons, costumes, oil paintings, and a Nordland fishing boat. There, too, are reproductions of the Nidaros Cathedral in Trondheim, Norway, and the Maihaugen Museum, farm models, a flag from the Fifteenth Wisconsin Regiment of the Civil War and other military objects, coins and paper currency, and various items of interest to the ethnologist and natural historian.

In 1931, a large three-story building in downtown Decorah, previously the Lutheran Publishing House, was placed at the disposal of the museum. In the next year, after remodeling, many of the museum's objects were moved into it. Exhibits showed, on the first floor, how people had lived in Norway, and, on the second, how the early pioneers lived in this country. This golden age for the museum came to an end with the death of Gjerset in 1936. His contribution in turning the museum into a modern institution was a lasting legacy to his fellow Norwegian Americans.

Acquisitions were also made in following years. From 1936 to 1937, Knute O. Eitrem was director, and Sigurd S. Reque served in this capacity from 1939 to 1947; he was succeeded by Inga Bredesen Norstog from 1947 to 1960. During the next four years, Oivind Hovde, Luther's librarian, was acting director, with Mrs. Ralph M. Olson as assistant.

A new departure was made in 1964, when, largely at the initiative of David T. Nelson and President E. D. Farwell of Luther College, the museum became a separate corporation under the name Norwegian-American Museum. Its certificate of incorporation was approved by the state of Iowa on October 26. Dr. Gunnar Gundersen of La Crosse, Wisconsin, was elected president, and Marion J. Nelson, professor of art and Scandinavian studies at the University of Minnesota, became director.

The new independent museum, which in 1969 adopted the additional name of Vesterheim (Home in the West), has gone forward with vigor. An illustrated quarterly newsletter has been mailed to interested persons since 1965, and in 1967 a non-voting membership was created. At present there are about 2,500 members.

The cataloguing of the museum's nearly 10,000 objects by the director and his wife, Lila Nelson, represents a valuable contribution. Even more impressive has been the expansion and renovation of facilities. In 1969 the board adopted as official policy a historical preservation program in the area of the museum building. Darrell D. Henning was hired as curator in 1970 and given the responsibility of creating an industrial division centering around the Decorah stone mill in the museum complex. In following years, the museum gradually acquired much of the property it intended to restore, and in 1970 it was also given the Norwegian Methodist church at nearby Washington Prairie, built in 1863–1868; this was restored and rededicated in 1973. The largest venture at present is the complete renovation of the old museum building, with the exterior restored to its appearance of 1877. This project will cost a quarter million dollars.

In addition, since 1967 the museum has co-operated with the Decorah community in arranging a Nordic Fest — a three-day folk and arts festival — which has become an annual event attracting large crowds. The museum has also conducted workshops in *rosemaling* (rose painting) and wood carving, with teachers from Norway.

The Vesterheim complex has thus become an institution of popular education, as well as a place for the serious scholar to gain insights into the past. Its exhibits and programs have provided avenues of understanding to the circumstances surrounding the lives of earlier generations. For many, a visit to the museum has represented a nostalgic and sentimental journey back to pioneer conditions. In the manner of similar immigrant institutions, it has generated pride in the Norwegian-American experience. The visual presentations have complemented the works of scholarship produced by the Historical Association. The shared responsibility to explain and to preserve the history of the Norwegian element in America has drawn these two institutions together and has furthered a spirit of co-operation during the past fifty years.

VI

THE ASSOCIATION'S ARCHIVES

THE early concern — expressed by the *bygdelag* and others — for a repository for documents pertaining to Norwegian-American life found a gradual solution with the coming of the Association. Without the preservation of such source materials, there can be no history. Expression was early given to the urgency of saving the precious story of migration, settlement, and adjustment reflected in letters, diaries, records of societies and churches, files of newspapers and other printed matter, as well as in the memories of a passing generation. When the archives plan of the *bygdelag* failed in 1914, hope was expressed that the new fireproof building of the Minnesota State Historical Society in St. Paul might become a central repository for the Norwegians. Theodore C. Blegen, in 1921 and later, spoke for such a possibility, adding that there already was a fair collection of Scandinavian materials in the Society. During the newspaper debate in 1924 for a historical organization, *Minneapolis Tidende* stressed editorially the advantages of adding to the archival collection in St. Paul instead of seeking a new location. Blegen sought the support of O. E. Rølvaag for this plan, but with little success.

At the organizing meeting in Northfield on October 6, 1925, the question of archives became a delicate one, as there existed collections of documents and records in several places other than in the Minnesota capital. Representatives from Wisconsin and North

Dakota especially opposed the St. Paul location. A diplomatic solution was reached in a resolution of support for "Archives in St. Paul, Luther College, St. Olaf College, Wisconsin State Historical Society and other places," as designated by the Association. The idea was to help existing repositories to carry forward their programs without financial support from the Norwegian-American Historical Association.

Subsequent developments, however, made the archives at St. Olaf College the Association's central collection. Many factors made it almost inevitable that it should be so. The enthusiastic support of L. W. Boe, the college's president and later vice president of the Association, gave significant impetus to this development. He supported Rølvaag in his work as the Association's secretary. The fact that the secretary's office was located at St. Olaf made it appear the major center of the organization's activity; according to the articles of incorporation, the secretary clearly was to have charge of the archives. Rooms provided by the college for documentary materials were approved at the first regular triennial meeting of the Association in Minneapolis in 1927. Rølvaag and J. Jørgen Thompson added to the existing sources by making Sunday excursions by automobile in the environs of Northfield; these trips were followed by long hours devoted to evaluating and organizing the collected materials. Like later secretaries, Rølvaag performed a labor of love, giving unstintingly of his dynamic energy to the task immediately at hand: corresponding, collecting, and classifying.

Thus, in 1932, when Dr. Carlton C. Qualey served as field agent, it seemed appropriate for the Association to authorize that the documents and books assembled by him be placed at St. Olaf College. Qualey had visited settlements in Minnesota, Wisconsin, Iowa, and Illinois, securing valuable materials and generally creating interest for the project of preserving records. Norwegian-born Sir Karl Knudsen of London, who had been knighted by the British for his services to the Allies during World War I, also took an interest in the Association and deposited money in a Norwegian bank to engage people in Norway to collect "America letters" and to search for information in maritime records and departmental files. Mrs. Gudrun Natrud of Oslo co-operated with Blegen in acquiring valuable documents and in preparing a calendar of Norwegian archival materials dealing with American history and migration. Dr. Gunnar J. Malmin had located significant sources in Norwegian libraries during the year 1923–1924, and in 1928–1929 Blegen spent time in Norway gathering "America letters" and other materials for his study of early Norwegian migration. These, in time, were deposited at St. Olaf College.

St. Olaf thereby came to be regarded as the official sheltering institution for the archives of the Association, and in reality it served as such. Little money, however, was expended by the Association on the collection, because, in Blegen's words, "with limited funds we have concentrated on one essential line, and that has been publication." J. Jørgen Thompson, dean of men and professor at St. Olaf, was assistant secretary from 1925, and, after Rølvaag's death in 1931, he became secretary and archivist, serving in this capacity until 1959. He fulfilled with dedication the tasks assigned to the secretary: corresponding, keeping the membership records, mailing out statements and receipting the paying of dues, and addressing and mailing to members all books published. The secretary served and serves as guide to visitors and as recruitment officer for new members. In his position as archivist, Thompson worked unselfishly to give the collection of books and documents a permanent place in the program of the Association.

As acquisitions were made and donations of materials accumulated, their proper processing and storing became urgent. In 1933, Agnes M. Larson of the St. Olaf history department, assisted by Esther Gulbrandson of the department of Norwegian, took over direct care of the 1,800 items then in the archives. The collection was augmented by donations from Rølvaag's private library of more than 350 books and pamphlets, about 1,000 items from the library of O. S. Johnson, farmer and amateur historian, and later by important donations of materials from the estates of D. G. Ristad, Laurence M. Larson, and other individuals who sought safekeeping for valuable materials. Alf Houkom, college librarian, worked to organize the archival holdings after he was appointed curator in 1936.

The Association's fifth triennial meeting in 1939 created a board of archives composed of Agnes M. Larson, chairman, Karen Larsen, and Jacob Hodnefield. Hodnefield became chairman in 1945. Professor O. M. Norlie and John Frohlin of Bayonne, New Jersey, also served on this board. The function of the board of archives was one of accession as well as organization. As the Association has not been able to finance a field agent on a permanent basis, appeals were made by the board for documents and other historical matter of interest. The favorable response by members and friends has been essential to the building of the archival collection.

In 1942 the archives occupied the entire seventh floor of the newly opened Ole E. Rølvaag Memorial Library on the St. Olaf campus. The materials, however, had not been properly catalogued. Easy reference to their contents was therefore impossible. As the consequence of a gift of $1,000 in 1945 by Magnus Bjorndal of Weehawken, New Jersey, the services of a part-time cataloguer were secured, and in 1947 the executive board appropriated another thousand dollars for the same purpose. The desire to put the archives in full working order was felt as a pressing need; an annual sum of $500 was therefore made available by the executive board. In 1952, Chrisma Dittmann was hired as part-time cataloguer, and she greatly improved the arrangement of the materials. Later, both donated and hired help by college students and faculty enhanced their quality and availability.

Finally, in 1959, St. Olaf greatly increased its support of the Association. The college librarian, speaking for President Clemens M. Granskou, presented the executive board with an offer to assume the management and organization of the archives. Books would become integrated with the college library, although remaining in the possession of the Association. Books and documents would now receive continuous professional care and be catalogued in accordance with highest accepted standards. The board unanimously accepted this generous offer.

At this time, Professor Lloyd Hustvedt, presently chairman of the department of Norwegian at St. Olaf, succeeded Dean Thompson as secretary and archivist. Great advances have been made during Hustvedt's tenure. In 1960, Beulah Folkedahl of Madison, Wisconsin, was hired to assist the college cataloguer in organizing the Association's collection. St. Olaf had paid for staff time earlier and also covered Miss Folkedahl's salary. When she assumed her duties, about 5,000 books had been catalogued and integrated with the college library; at least 1,000 remained to be processed.

More complex and time-consuming was the task of cataloguing the vast collection of unpublished manuscript material. Such work is less dramatic than research and writing, which eventually result in publication, but nevertheless it is essential to the communication of history. Professional descriptions of documents in harmony with Library of Congress specifications were prepared. A forty-year backlog of collected documents and papers had been catalogued by 1966; these included the large O. M. Norlie collection, which required an entire year of Miss Folkedahl's time. When she died in 1971, Miss Folkedahl, archivist from 1966, had organized the holdings and prepared an index of the descriptions, thereby making possible a cross reference to the contents of the archives. In September, 1974, there were 744 individual collections ranging in size from 42 file boxes and 23,220 items for American Relief to Norway to those with only a few documents. The total archival holdings consist of 226,324 items. These figures, however, are somewhat misleading, as an item might be a manuscript of several hundred pages or a letter on a single sheet. In addition, there are many boxes of documents not yet properly catalogued.

The Association's archives have thus become the foremost collection of materials pertaining to Norwegian-American history — accessible to scholar and general investigator alike. In 1966, the Association moved to new quarters on the ground level of a new wing to the Rølvaag Library. Office furnishings, a gift from a furniture manufacturer, Mr. Arne J. Opsahl of Hamar, Norway, are in contemporary Scandinavian design. The papers were then transferred into new, smaller, and more accessible documentary file cases. Miss Charlotte Jacobson, associate professor of English and assistant librarian, donated half the fund, $500, required for the purchase of the new cases. In the fall of 1974, after retiring from the college faculty, Miss Jacobson entered directly into the service of the Association to catalogue and index the accessions of recent years and to perform the other tasks of the curator.

No student of the Norwegian-American experience can afford to pass the archives by. To the person writing a family history, the 150,000 or more newspaper clippings containing personal biographies, mainly obituaries — which was begun in 1913 by A. A. Rowberg, then editor of the *Northfield Independent* — are an indispensable tool. They provide a beginning for a special genealogical department, envisioned already in 1938. Many donations of copies of family histories, as well as the increasing number of requests for information about relatives, attest to a growing preoccupation with genealogy.

The archives also contain the papers and writings of many personalities — editors and writers like Waldemar Ager, Rasmus Bjørn Anderson, Hjalmar Hjorth Boyesen, Hans A. Foss, Nicolay A. Grevstad, Carl G. O. Hansen, Kristofer Janson, Simon Johnson, Knud Langeland, Jon Norstog, Kristian Prestgard, O. E. Rølvaag, N. N. Rønning, Peer O. Strømme, and Marcus Thrane; poets like Julius B. Baumann and O. A. Buslett; churchmen like L. W. Boe, Nils Brandt, Claus L. Clausen, J.W.C. Dietrichson, Elling Eielsen, Helge Høverstad, G. M. Bruce, Rasmus Meland, D. G. Ristad, Carl K. Solberg, and Oscar A. Tingelstad; educators and artists like F. Melius Christiansen, John Dahle, Knut Gjerset, Theodore Jorgenson, Carl L. Lokke, O. M. Norlie, Andrew A. Veblen; politicians and labor leaders like Andrew Furuseth, Nils P. Haugen, Knute Nelson, and Knud Wefald; industrialists and men of business like Ole Evinrude, John A. Johnson, and Birger Osland; engineers like Magnus Bjorndal and Magnus Swenson; a military hero like Colonel Hans C. Heg; contributors from many other walks of life such as O. O. Enestvedt, Torkel Oftelie, Olaf E. Ray, A. O. Serum, John Storseth, and many others. These were leaders in the immigrant community; their observations and the records of their lives contained in diaries, correspondence, newspaper clippings, articles, and published volumes are fascinating avenues to an understanding of developments within Norwegian America.

The archives also have census returns, histories of counties, church publications and reports, the records of many academies, business schools, and colleges founded by the immigrants, as well as the minutes and other documents of organizations such as the Arne Garborg Klubb in Chicago, the Norwegian Society of America, and the many bygdelag. There one can find the records of benevolent societies — hospitals, orphanages, and old people's homes — and of special activities and celebrations such as the Norse-American Centennial of 1925 and Aid to Norway during World War II.

In addition to novels, collections of poetry, magazines, pamphlets, and similar materials published by Norwegian Americans, the archives contain substantial files of immigrant newspapers such as *Skandinaven*, *Decorah-Posten*, *Samfundet*, *Fædrelandet*, *Minneapolis Tidende*, *Amerika*, and *Washington-Posten*. There, too, are the materials used in the preparation of Theodore C. Blegen's volumes, a large collection of "America letters," and the sources employed by Kenneth O. Bjork in preparing his study of the engineers and the story of migration to the west coast, and also many other significant documents, photographs, and illustrations. Over the years, a number of doctoral dissertations and master's theses dealing with immigrant topics have come to the archives. The student of any phase of Norwegian-American history could well begin his search there. A number of prominent scholars, graduate students, and creative writers have found useful information as well as inspiration in the Association's repository.

The pressures on the secretary's office have increased with the growing attention the archives have gained nationally. The listing of the Association's collection in the *Union Catalog of Manuscripts* in 1969 by the Library of Congress, mention in directories, bibliographies, travel guides, and books on how to trace your ancestors have stimulated requests for services from publishing firms, authors, and individuals which exceed the scope of the limited staff. A significant future development would thus seem to be an expansion of services by an enlarged salaried staff and a paid director.

VII

THE ASSOCIATION'S MEMBERSHIP

OVER the past half-century the Norwegian-American Historical Association has firmly established itself in a position of leadership. Its primary purpose has been to communicate to a wide public the history created by those who came from Norway and by their descendants in this country. At present, 111 libraries have standing orders for all Association publications, 40 historical and other publishing societies have exchange relationships with it, and 37 or more journals receive complimentary review copies of its publications. These arrangements provide a large audience for the Association and assure its books a wide distribution.

The support of devoted and faithful members — those who stay with the Association for many years — represents its major strength. Their dues, in addition to donations and receipts from book sales, have been the mainstay of all activity. Unfortunately, membership has been much smaller than might have been hoped, or even expected, in light of the many persons of Norwegian birth or extraction in this country. It is difficult to explain why more have not found the goals and performance of the Association worthy of their support. The organization is, of course, itself partly to blame. It has never engaged in a vigorous solicitation, nor given wide and general publicity to its efforts, and it has not been able to afford the services of a field agent to recruit members. It has often had to rely on interested members and friendly newspapers to spread the word.

In spite of a distinguished record covering a period of fifty years, the Association still remains unknown to the majority of Americans of Norwegian descent.

There are four classes of members in the Association: associate, sustaining, patron, and life. The first pay dues of $7, the second, $12; the patron member gives $25, and a life membership is acquired by one payment of $100. In addition, since 1970 there has been a patron life membership of $250. Institutional and memorial memberships of $100 have a duration of twenty-five years. All classes of members enjoy the same rights, and virtually every publication has been mailed to all members, regardless of category. The class of associates, in particular, has thus received a substantial return on investment. In the total picture, a most encouraging development has been the gift of life memberships to children, grandchildren, nieces, and nephews by staunch supporters of the Association.

A study of membership statistics provides an enlightening insight into the Association's growth and its ups and downs. The first three years witnessed a phenomenal increase as enthusiasm for the organization was generated. By Christmas, 1925, almost 200 persons had joined. In 1926 — much of the growth occurring even before the first publication was distributed — the membership figure stood at 745, and in the following year it peaked at 842. During the next years, there was a high rate of cancellation; the lukewarm dropped out, according to J. Jørgen Thompson, because the Association was not sufficiently "Norwegian," did not give room for filiopietistic writings, and issued all publications in English. Some also shied away because they harbored antiacademic sentiments or desired more "popular" literature. The depression of the 1930s added to the problem: in 1934, only 527 members paid their dues — a low point in support of the Association.

Membership grew slowly thereafter. In 1939, 150 new members were added, and a vigorous drive in 1941 brought in 308 more; in all, there were 929 members. Years of growth have usually been followed by numerous cancellations; in the next year, as many as 99 dropped out. Cancellations were also heavy in 1949 and 1951. These declines may be explained in part by an increase in associate dues — which from the beginning had been at the low figure of $2

— first to $3 and then to $5. The decreases might also have resulted from a lagging interest in national diversity caused by the political and social pressures of the times. In 1955, total membership was only 721.

A second drive in 1958 brought the membership to 834, with 173 new persons entering their names on the Association's roster. Only a handful of years have witnessed additions of more than a hundred. The Association passed the thousand mark in 1964. Since then the total number of members has fluctuated from a little over 1,100 in 1966 to about 1,000 at the end of 1974.

The increase in associate dues to present levels in January, 1971, caused some to drop their membership. Cancellations in recent years, however, have been relatively light, as is demonstrated by the gradual increase in length of individual memberships. At present, the average person stays with the Association 6.5 years. This figure indicates both those who cancel after one year and the large number who remain with the Association for the rest of their lives once they have made a commitment. There are still charter members from 1925 and others who joined after learning of the organization only in the following year.

The members are individuals from all walks of life. This fact gives the Association strength and provides spokesmen in all sections of the Norwegian-American population — as well as among other ethnic groups. By the end of 1974, a total of 4,212 individuals had appeared on the Association's membership rolls. The professional identity of 1,498 of these is known. The teaching profession has been represented by 266; ministers have numbered 140, students, 114, businessmen, 227, bankers, 16, lawyers, 68, doctors, 52, housewives, 45, tradesmen, 84, farmers, 42, and politicians, 67.

The Association has never been a regional organization, although understandably it has been easiest to recruit close to its headquarters. There are members in forty-two of the fifty states and in the District of Columbia. Individuals and institutions in seven foreign countries also have joined. In September, 1974, Minnesota had 269 members, Illinois, 127, Wisconsin, 93, California, 66, Iowa, 56, Washington, 50, New York, 31, North Dakota and Texas, 25 each, and South Dakota, 17. Norway had 34 members and Canada, 6.

The figures indicate a wide geographical distribution, but also considerable room for an increase in support.

The organizing body in 1925 set up a system of local vice presidents for various regions of Norwegian settlement. Their function was to create interest and recruit new members for the Association. On the whole, the over-all impact of their work has been minimal. In the late 1930s, C. Martin Alsager, vice president for Chicago, and R. A. Nestos, representing North Dakota, nevertheless had good results in membership drives. The recruitment of members has been on a personal level, by invitations from the office of the secretary, by direct contacts, and by gift memberships. There has also been modest publicity through paid advertising in the press, mass mailings to groups with a potential interest, and informative talks at Norwegian-American gatherings.

The launching of a newsletter in November, 1934, prepared and edited for the most part by the secretary, has proved an effective means of communication with members. The newsletter has stimulated interest and kept members informed, but it has appeared irregularly. Most issues have contained reports of triennial and executive meetings, lists of new members and donations, reports by the editor, additions to the archives, and other material pertaining to a variety of activities. A more frequent distribution would be desirable.

VIII

THE FINANCES

MEMBERS have often expressed the idea that the strength of the Association derives from the co-operative efforts and sacrifices of scholars and men of the business and professional world. The history of the organization demonstrates how such a united effort has come to fruition through an extensive program of publication. The effort to produce valuable works of history — with emphasis consistently on quality and not quantity — has thus been intimately interwoven with the struggle to provide sufficient funds. Time and again, we have seen how money was forthcoming once there was a worthy manuscript ready for publication.

Birger Osland, one of the three incorporators of the Association, exemplified a high sense of stewardship of the Association's resources. Osland served as assistant treasurer from 1925 to 1930, and then as treasurer until 1951. He was a steward of such magnitude that no editorial task seemed impossible. Drawing on his experience with the company he founded in Chicago in 1911 — Birger Osland and Company, Investments — he invested funds with caution and skill and donated generously and often to the treasury. When he retired, his associates said of him: "By example and precept [he] has given direction to the Association during a quarter century of development and expansion."

Not even the depression of the 1930s significantly halted the publication program. In 1933, however, an overly ambitious editorial activity more than depleted available funds, and some projects had to be postponed — but not for long. "Vigor, vigor, and yet more vigor in the work of the Association" expressed the managing editor's views that year when he commented on Osland's ability to cope with the shortage of funds. Throughout its existence, the Association has enjoyed the services of men who have displayed great capability and care as custodians of the funds at its disposition. They have invested money wisely and safely, and it has yielded good returns.

An early objective was to establish a permanent fund to secure future operations. It was created in 1928 at a February meeting of the executive board in Chicago. The ambitious goal of $100,000 has not yet been achieved. In 1936, the name of this permanent endowment was changed to honor one of the major promoters in the early years: The Ole Edvart Rølvaag Memorial Fund. In that year it had $14,319.68, built up from donations, bequests, life and memorial membership dues, reinvested interest premiums, and, until 1933, from the sale of books. In 1938 the Rølvaag Fund totaled about $18,000.

All monies of the Association have been invested in bonds, treasury notes, and stocks. The pressures of publication during the Great Depression caused a change in determining the size of the Rølvaag Fund. Only life and memorial membership dues and specified donations eventually were included — a fact that reduced its worth to only $8,855 in 1950. From this time, it has grown to more than $25,000.

The Association established a second permanent fund at the fifteenth triennial meeting in Chicago in June, 1969, to honor its first managing editor. The Theodore C. Blegen Fellowship Fund, on the initiative of Professor Bjork, was designed to assist the publication program by providing financial aid to authors engaged in the completion of manuscripts deemed suitable for publication. The target was a sum of $30,000, from which both interest and some principal might be used. The executive board donated $7,300, some members gave substantial gifts, and many others have contributed smaller amounts. In 1972, Dr. Gunnar Gundersen, then president, pledged to match all future contributions. As a result, he has given several thousand dollars, and the fund has exceeded its original goal. As yet, no allocations have been made from it.

Current operations are financed by an expense fund. Its major source of revenue has been the dues of other than life members. From 1925 to 1950, $47,242.52 were paid in associate and sustaining dues; these same sources provided another $63,985 by 1966, and by the end of 1974, a total of about $289,546. The first volume of *Studies and Records* in 1926 printed an invitation to make bequests to the Association, and this practice has been continued in the series. A total of $43,085.10 had been added to the treasury through bequests by 1966, and more than $55,000 by the end of 1974. In the first twenty-five years, a little over $47,000 was spent on publications. Significantly, in the next sixteen years an additional $64,000 were expended for this purpose. The expense fund, which has also increased by gains and interest on investments, in 1975 stands at about $28,000. It is remarkable that about eighty percent of all expenditures have been directly related to the publishing of books. Because of dedicated and donated talent, the Association has always received considerable return from its financial resources.

A special fund was set up and gifts were solicited for the purpose of researching, writing, and printing this fiftieth-anniversary history of the Association. A sum of $2,000 was raised by a generous matching gift of half this amount by Dr. Arthur Davidson, president of Wagner College on Staten Island, and the rest by appeals to the entire membership.

IX

EDITORIAL LEADERSHIP

THEODORE C. BLEGEN, professor of history and later dean of the graduate school in the University of Minnesota, served as the Association's managing editor from its beginning to 1960 — a period of thirty-five years. He accepted the position with a preconceived publication program, and he strictly adhered to the highest standards of selection, writing, and editing. As a result, the Association has avoided the inherent danger of yielding to easy solutions and has turned a deaf ear to the special pleading that has characterized some ethnic historical societies. He was a dynamic and vital force in earning the remarkable reputation that the Association has enjoyed. It became a model to be emulated by other immigrant groups, some of which are only presently beginning to record their history in this country.

Blegen's association with the Minnesota Historical Society proved of great value as a preparation for guiding the editorial policy of the new organization. His qualities of leadership and his wide understanding and appreciation of all aspects of human endeavor placed him in the front among local and state historians. He had the unique ability of raising the commonplace and ordinary to high levels of significance and to give it a proper perspective. He drew up a long and valuable bibliography in the history of immigration and in other fields, served as editor of *Minnesota History*, and was a teacher of history. He succeeded Solon J. Buck as superintendent of the Minnesota Historical Society, having gained valuable insights into the arts of editing and meticulous research from his earlier apprenticeship under his predecessor.

Knut Gjerset and Kristian Prestgard, the two other members of the original editorial board, were in harmony with Blegen in advocating sound judgment and professional procedures in building the Association's publication program. The three men did not always agree on details, but careful and sincere debate, as indicated in correspondence stored in the Association's archives, ultimately resulted in wise decisions.

As policy was formulated, many issues had to be dealt with early. A suggestion that additional revenue be obtained by including advertisements in publications was rejected after the advice of scholars and friends was sought. Consul E. H. Hobe of St. Paul felt that advertising would so reduce quality that he offered to raise the money lost by omitting it. The editors also asked for advice in establishing high standards of professional printing, editing, and book design and production. The best historical journals were used as models. The Association stayed clear of controversial issues related to such matters as the Kensington Stone and the Leif Ericson discovery of North America. Similarly, it refused to become a church history society, as some had feared it might do, but it has given full attention to the role of religion in the Norwegian-American story.

The broad approach, the genuine interest in all facets of immigrant life, was stated early by Blegen, and it was repeated and sustained over the years. Dr. Kenneth O. Bjork, as new managing editor, gave clear expression to this dominant editorial attitude in a speech he delivered in the 1960s: "In thinking of these matters and of editorial problems . . . we must never forget that our ultimate purpose is to tell the story of the men and women who tilled the soil of the New World, who went down to sea in ships, who worked the mines and machines of our industrial plant. We are mindful of those who cared for the sick in body and spirit, who edited newspapers and magazines, who wrote poems and novels, and who dreamed dreams of a better America. We think of pioneers — those who opened up new areas of settlement, who invented new techniques in production, built bridges, tunnels, skyscrapers, and other structures, who harnessed the force of electricity, who started and nurtured schools, churches and political movements. We are reminded of those who opened shops, directed business enterprises, practiced law, or responded to the call of duty when danger threatened our country. And we do not forget the men and women whose lives were undramatic and unsung, or were marked by frustration and defeat. For we are committed to telling the whole story of a transplanted people that is now deeply rooted in America — one small part of the millions who made the great Atlantic crossing. If we do this imaginatively, if we do it thoroughly and well, we will meet a special obligation to this great land that we call our home, and we will contribute largely to the growth of its maturing culture.''

Other scholars have also served with distinction on the editorial board. The list includes Professors Laurence M. Larson, Marcus L. Hansen, Carlton C. Qualey, Einar Haugen, Paul Knaplund, Martin B. Ruud, Clarence A. Clausen, and Peter A. Munch, Carl L. Lokke, and Erik J. Friis. They have been outstanding men, each in his own right, and have contributed substantially to the selection and acquisition of publishable material. Professors Larson and Qualey also accepted direct responsibility for individual volumes of the *Studies and Records* series, as did Dr. Bjork, who in 1960 succeeded Blegen as the second managing editor.

Professor Bjork, since joining the faculty of St. Olaf in 1937, has been actively engaged in the work of the Association. He has been a member of the editorial board since 1939, and, except for leaves of absence as guest lecturer and researcher, has had his academic career at the college. He has participated widely both in campus affairs and in a large number of outside professional and public activities, and has been a productive writer. He has carried on the traditions and high standards set by Blegen during his long tenure as editor. The Association has thus been in the position of being able to attract men of scholarly integrity, who have donated their talent and time to meeting the challenge accepted at its inception fifty years ago.

Assistance in editing early became a necessity; the work could not be carried out wholly by men occupied in other full-time positions. The duties of the editor could easily require a person's total working capacity. Financial support of the editor's office, however, has been limited to payment to assistant editors and typists. All other labor has been donated.

X

IN SUPPORT OF RESEARCH

A GREAT deal has been accomplished by adding to the manuscript collections in the archives. Even more significant has been the research attending the preparation of manuscripts. Only rarely has any kind of financial remuneration been possible for this purpose; the scholars have contributed their services free of charge. Blegen, in reviewing twenty-five years as the Association's managing editor, stated: "Author after author in the whole range of our work has turned over to me for publication his or her manuscript without payment for the months and often years of patient work that have gone into it." In this spirit of co-operation, they have, as Blegen continued, "matched with the gifts of their minds the financial gifts that have done so much to make our program possible."

Publications have not fallen like ripe fruit into the lap of the editor. Contributors, both those with established reputations and those who have been less experienced workers in the field, have been sought out and invited to present articles or to undertake major research projects. No one, of course, has been given a promise of publication in advance. As Blegen described the task of the editor: "Most of our production has come from stimulation and encouragement, suggestions of things worth doing, earnest urging, conferences, letters." The only incentive has been the prospect of publication if studies are found worthy by the editorial board. The extensive letter writing, prodding, and guidance involved at times have made the editor's office appear a graduate seminar by correspondence.

Although the publication program of the Association by and large has been developed on the basis of noncompensated voluntary service, occasionally it has been possible to free a qualified scholar from other duties and commitments by granting him a fellowship or giving him some aid in meeting expenses. Much valuable work has been accomplished in such cases, and it is a pity that not more assistance has been possible. Scholars, tied down with heavy teaching loads, college committee work, and community participation, have only spare hours in which to pursue research and writing. Without substantial grants and travel allowances, they cannot hope to investigate and utilize essential sources. When the Association has been able to lend support, the funds have derived from interested individuals.

Knut Gjerset was able to devote considerable time away from his teaching duties at Luther College to research his two studies on the Norwegian sailors in the United States. His extensive travels to assemble the necessary information were supported by a number of individuals who contributed money. His first book on the sailors on the Great Lakes had the financial support of Birger Osland and the first treasurer of the Association, O. M. Oleson, a businessman in Dodge City, Iowa.

His second study, published in 1933, was, in a sense, a sequel to his first volume, covering the Atlantic seaboard; a number of people in the East contributed to support Gjerset's research efforts. The donors were A. N. Rygg, Charles E. Larsen, Sigurd J. Arnesen, all of Brooklyn; Elias A. Cappelen-Smith, Nelson B. Nelson, and the Todd Shipyards Corporation of New York; Frederic Shaefer of Pittsburgh and Magnus Swenson of Madison, Wisconsin.

Both of Bjork's major works, requiring extensive travel, prolonged periods away from teaching duties, and a loss of salary, were supported by funds given to the Association. His first study on the Norwegian engineers in America required a leave of absence for the academic year 1940–1941, and the Association was able to grant him a fellowship for that year. His research on the west coast was supported mainly by Olaf Halvorson of Huntington Park, California. Theodore C. Blegen was made a fellow of the Association, and in 1939–1940 he was able to devote full time to completing his second volume on Norwegian migration. Foundations have also recognized the significance of these and other projects by conferring grants in support of them. A fine example was the aid given Agnes M. Larson by the Gisholt John A. Johnson Foundation of Madison, Wisconsin, when she prepared a biography of the immigrant businessman whose name is honored by the organization.

At a later date, the Association made available through close co-operation with Bygdelagenes Fellesraad (Council of Bygdelags) funds to assist Dr. Odd S. Lovoll in his study of the *bygdelag* movement in this country. Clearly, judging from the returns in the form of important scholarly works, the Association needs to do even more to enable scholars to devote full time to research. As Blegen stated in 1950, "Many things we dreamed of have not been done because we lacked energy or time or means or success in our hunt for others to do them or join us in doing them." The creation of the fund now bearing Blegen's name is a step — but only a step — in the right direction.

XI

NORWEGIAN-AMERICAN STUDIES

THE Association has published twenty-nine volume-length mono-graphs and translations of sources, as well as twenty-six collections of shorter primary and secondary materials relating to Norwegian migration to the New World and to the life of the transplanted Norwegians in America. Essays and documents have been included in the *Studies and Records* series, which was launched in 1926. In 1931, with volume 6, the title was changed to *Norwegian-American Studies and Records*, and with volume 11, in 1940, the editors abandoned the early pamphlet form in favor of a hard-covered book format. Volume 21, in 1962, appeared with the abbreviated title *Norwegian-American Studies* and an altered design.

The original plan had apparently been for an annual publication, and so in early years the volumes in the series were referred to as "yearbooks." It also called for a quarterly magazine to replace the annuals. The program adopted later of issuing irregularly valuable source materials, together with articles, has provided greater flexibility and permitted more exacting editorial standards than would a fixed annual or quarterly publication date, and the Association has been well served by the new arrangement.

Changes in appearance have not affected the basic content of the *Studies* series. The great store of information that it contains — often strong on interpretation — on varied phases of the immigrant story, in addition to the biographical listings after 1930, offers fascinating reading for anyone and a wide-ranging presentation for the scholar. From 1962, the volumes have also commented on sources in the archives. Collectively, in the twenty-six volumes, there are more than 5,500 pages. Although the Association has never emphasized quantity over quality, the sheer bulk of printed material nevertheless calls for respect.

Before volume 1 in the series was distributed to the members, both impatience and apprehension had been expressed concerning the first fruit of the long-awaited society. Its 175 pages contained an essay on health conditions among the settlers, a study of the Norwegian Quakers in 1825, a presentation of the famous words of admonition against emigration by Bishop Jacob Neuman, and several other translated pieces. A distinguished Harvard historian, A. M. Schlesinger, wrote to Blegen after receiving the volume: "I wish to congratulate you heartily upon Volume One of the Studies and Records of the NAHA . . . for its format and contents, above all, the design of studying in detail and from a scholarly point of view the place of this racial stock in the American situation."

On the same occasion, the *American Historical Review* expressed this sentiment: "The new society has a rich and important field and is entitled to a hearty welcome." Similar cordial endorsements came from *Current History, Tidens Tegn* of Oslo, *Minnesota History*, the *Iowa Journal of History*, and other publications, and from individuals.

It is not possible to cover adequately the materials contained in the twenty-six volumes, nor to give a complete evaluation of their impact and reception both within and outside the academic community. Sample comments made by qualified reviewers may, however, present an idea of the broad scope and the high quality of the *Studies* series. George M. Stephenson, professor of history in the University of Minnesota, had this to say about volume 3, which had a number of translated sources but also contained a study of the Icelandic communities in America and an appraisal of the historical value of church records: "Each contributor to this volume has made a 'contribution' to history; and when a *magnum opus* on American immigration is planned — an event the editor thinks is near at hand — the writer will make levies under each caption."

With volume 7, in 1933, the *Mississippi Valley Historical Re-*

view (presently the *Journal of American History*) found the Association "the most active historical society among immigrant groups." The same journal, in judging the next volume in 1934, thought it had "reached a higher standard both as to its appearance as well as its contents." When volume 9 appeared in 1936, the historian O. Fritiof Ander maintained, also in the *Review*, that "in the main this volume . . . conforms to the high standard set by its editor." With other scholarly contributions, this volume included the sweepingly interpretive essay "Immigration and Puritanism," by Marcus L. Hansen.

Volume 10 published findings by Einar Haugen on "Language and Immigration," and the next issue, in 1940, provided a personal and revealing picture of O. E. Rølvaag's work for the Association written by Professor Kenneth O. Bjork. *The Lutheran Herald* welcomed the latter volume with enthusiasm in the extreme. "I cannot praise too highly the excellent, interesting, and instructive publication," the reviewer remarked.

The *Studies* of 1941, containing more than 200 pages, evoked the following reaction from the *Wisconsin Magazine of History:* "This volume of ten articles devoted principally to the social and cultural aspects of Norwegian-American history will prove instructive to the reader with a limited background of such history, enlightening to the most advanced student, and unusually entertaining to all." There were annual publications of the series also in the next three years. In 1943, Professor Ander, speaking in the *Survey of Current Literature* about volume 13, maintained: "To imagine that a closer familiarity with *Norwegian-American Studies and Records* would be pertinent only to those interested in immigration is to deprive oneself of the use of an important historical source."

Volume 16, edited by Kenneth O. Bjork and appearing in 1950, is devoted to settlement on the Pacific coast — a preview of Bjork's findings for his volume on migration to this region. The reader is taken from the pioneer Hvistendahl mission to San Francisco, across the Oregon and Washington Territory, and into the gold fields of Klondike and Alaska. "The NAHA may well feel proud of the contributions they have been making to historiography in America, and their sixteenth volume is a creditable addition," the *British Columbia Historical Quarterly* said of it.

Professor Carlton C. Qualey edited volume 19, published in 1956 in honor of Blegen; it included the managing editor's significant chapter, "The Immigrant Image of America," from *Land of Their Choice*, as the lead article. From 1960, Bjork has been the Association's editor. In reviewing volume 22 in 1965, Erik J. Friis made the following comment in the *American-Scandinavian Review:* "It . . . demonstrates anew the vitality of the research and writing carried out today in the field of Norwegian immigrant history."

The twenty-first volume of 1961 exceeded 300 pages in length; subsequent volumes have been averaging about this size. Scholarship and an ever-wider range of focus have characterized them. Appropriately, the reviewer in the *Pacific Northwest Quarterly* made the following observation in 1967 about volume 23, edited by Qualey: "For nearly fifty years the saga of the migrant has been told and retold in the publications of the Norwegian-American Historical Association, and yet there is always something new."

The same sentiment was expressed in the *Journal of American History* in its review of volume 25 in 1972: "Quality as well as format will place this twenty-fifth volume . . . on the shelf smartly alongside its sturdy predecessors reaching back to 1926. Kenneth O. Bjork and his assistants in the NAHA are good custodians of a distinguished tradition infused by the scholarship of such men as Theodore C. Blegen and Knut Gjerset."

The Association is justifiably proud of the twenty-six books in this series, the last published in 1974. They represent significant contributions to knowledge. The comments quoted above illustrate the wide appeal and the depth of response that the series has generated.

XII

THE TRAVEL AND DESCRIPTION SERIES

THE early editorial program was designed to include a number of series, each with a distinct character and objective. The Travel and Description Series was the first to materialize in specific publication. To date, eight volumes have appeared — a total of 1,336 pages; they consist mainly of translated materials, appropriately introduced and annotated.

The first volume appeared late in 1926 and introduced the so-called "America books." They were emigrant guidebooks which attempted to present conditions, prospects,and hardships in the New World — often as viewed by compatriots who had made the crossing. These books caused many to leave their homes and follow the trail of the earlier settlers. *Ole Rynning's True Account of America* had been published in 1838 in Norway. The Association printed the original text, a complete English translation, an introduction, and appropriate notes. This plan of publication was arrived at after some debate, but it established a pattern. The shorter *Peter Testman's Account of His Experiences in North America*, issued by the Association the following year, had first appeared in Norway in 1839, and it was presented by the Association in the same manner as the Rynning book. Both volumes were translated, edited, and prefaced by Blegen.

In 1847 and 1848, the Norwegian scholar Ole Munch Raeder had been sent by his government to study the jury system in the United States. A series of his informal letters were later printed in *Den Norske Rigstidende*. Munch Raeder was an observant student both of American life generally and of his countrymen who had migrated. His impressions were collected, translated, and edited by Gunnar J. Malmin and brought together in one volume, published in 1929 under the title *America in the Forties: The Letters of Ole Munch Raeder*.

Another bundle of "America letters," written by a Norwegian minister in pioneer Wisconsin, was brought out in 1947 as *Frontier Parsonage: The Letters of Olaus Fredrik Duus, Norwegian Pastor in Wisconsin, 1855–1858*. The insight given in these letters into his activities shows him to have been, in addition to a minister of the gospel, a farmer, a teacher, a land speculator, and even an amateur practitioner of medicine. He was a critical observer of the America he knew, but he gave vivid descriptions of life among the Norwegian Americans, their longing for the old homeland, their crude frontier existence, and their need for the services and leadership of a clergyman. The last volume in the series, published in 1973 as *A Pioneer Churchman: J. W. C. Dietrichson in Wisconsin, 1844–1850*, was edited and introduced in some detail by Professor E. Clifford Nelson; it expounds on the role of the minister in pioneer times. The book includes Dietrichson's *Travel Narrative* and *Parish Journal*; together they show how a stern and authoritarian personality attempted to create an ordered church among the immigrants. Although imperious in his actions, Dietrichson showed remarkable sympathy for the underprivileged and had an observant if critical eye for conditions in America.

The more common touch was presented in *Frontier Mother: The Letters of Gro Svendsen*. Translated and edited by Pauline Farseth and Blegen, it appeared in 1950. The volume presents Gro Svendsen through her letters to Norway over the period 1861–1877, and deals mainly with conditions in her Iowa dwelling. We follow her on the trek from Norway and inland to the American Middle West, and witness the founding of a frontier home and the rearing of a large family. The book is a memorable portrait of a pioneer woman and a valuable record of early life and hardships in America.

In volume 6, *The Lady with The Pen: Elise Wærenskjold in*

Texas, we meet another fascinating and proud frontier woman, one who settled in Texas. As the title suggests, Mrs. Wærenskjold was a dedicated writer who recorded her impressions in the period 1852 to 1895 in letters to a variety of people, both here and in the homeland. As many of them were printed in newspapers, she became the best known Norwegian in Texas. Professor Clarence A. Clausen edited the documents, which had been translated by the Verdandi Study Club of Minneapolis, and wrote a comprehensive introduction to them. The book, published in 1961, was the first under the general editorship of Kenneth O. Bjork. The *Southwestern Historical Quarterly* wrote of it: "The idea to bring out such a book as this is most commendable, and the NAHA deserves credit for sponsoring what turns out to be a first class publication." And indeed the letters are a valuable source for the social historian and an intimate account of the personal lives of those who settled on the frontier.

In 1965, the Association published *Klondike Saga: The Chronicle of a Minnesota Gold Mining Company*, by Carl L. Lokke. It is an engrossing tale of a group of men who sought their fortunes in the Klondike and Alaskan gold fields. Its only disappointment for the reader is that the argonauts were unsuccessful. *The Pacific Historical Review* gave the book this recommendation: "The volume is a refreshing departure from the usual specific account. . . . The sense of adventure and excitement does not suffer from Lokke's scholarship and temperate tone." These volumes thus provide vivid insights and colorful impressions of the conditions, the drama, and the excitement attending the lives of many who set out from the Old World to make homes and create a future for themselves and their children on this side of the Atlantic.

XIII

SPECIAL PUBLICATIONS

ONE of the early objectives of the Association was to publish "monographs and other works dealing with Norwegian-American history, literature, art, and culture." They would constitute a Special Publications series. At present, it includes eighteen publications comprising more than 6,000 pages. The works cover a vast area of knowledge and constitute some of the major contributions of the Association.

Knut Gjerset produced two volumes on the sailors: *Norwegian Sailors on the Great Lakes: A Study in the History of American Inland Transportation*, 1928, the first book in the series, and, in 1933, *Norwegian Sailors in American Waters: A Study in the History of Maritime Activity on the Eastern Seaboard*. His writings present much detail, list the names of hundreds of sailors, and relate their contributions to the maritime profession in this country. The material was painstakingly collected at considerable personal sacrifice by the author.

The Association was fortunate when Theodore C. Blegen agreed to have his studies of Norwegian migration published under its impress. *Norwegian Migration to America, 1825–1860* (1931) and *Norwegian Migration to America: The American Transition* (1941) became classics, and were recognized as such from the start. The *Wisconsin Magazine of History* said of the first volume: "We believe that no national group that has moved from Europe to America in the nineteenth century has found a historian who has dealt more adequately with the causes, facts, and results of its transfer than Dr. Blegen and that his book is epoch-making in its thoroughness and comprehensiveness."

The *Lutheran Herald* maintained that the book was "a classic and should be found in every university, college, and public library." The level of scholarship attained by Blegen in this first volume dispelled any doubt that might have existed as to the seriousness and depth of commitment of those who pursued the stated goals of the Association. The second volume was anticipated with excitement, and the *American Historical Review* noted, after its publication, that when "other national groups in the United States find themselves historians of equal stature, future Americans will be able to understand their origins."

Blegen was also responsible for *The Civil War Letters of Colonel Hans Christian Heg*, which included a historical introduction of this hero of the Civil War period. The book, published in 1936, had been ready for the printer the year before, when a second collection of letters was uncovered, larger than the original; a reworking became necessary to include the new material. Most of the personal papers of Colonel Heg, however, had been destroyed. Ignorance of the historical significance of papers by survivors has caused the destruction of other priceless records as well.

An important supplement to Blegen's two volumes on migration, and a vital contribution in itself, appeared in 1939 with Professor Carlton C. Qualey's *Norwegian Settlement in the United States*. This work utilized quantitative methods to trace patterns of Norwegian settlement as it moved westward from the Atlantic seaboard. Dr. Qualey's book is indispensable for scholars and others.

A comprehensive work on west coast settlement, Kenneth O. Bjork's *West of the Great Divide: Norwegian Migration to the Pacific Coast, 1847–1893*, which was published in 1958, completes the volumes on migration and settlement. The *Pacific Historical Review* reviewed it by stating: "Norwegian migration to the Far West is a colorful and important story. . . . This tremendous work of research and writing thrills a reader of Scandinavian descent and fills a void which has plagued historians of immigration." A comment from the *Utah Historical Quarterly* is also of interest:

"Professor Bjork's full and fair treatment of the Mormons is typical of the way he combines large perspective and revealing detail in the rest of the narrative."

Bjork had already established his credentials with his pioneering work on "a migration of skills" entitled *Saga in Steel and Concrete: Norwegian Engineers in America*, published in 1947. "Here is an extremely well told story about our engineers and architects, an elite one might say, among Norwegian immigrants, which perhaps is generally less known than other groups," the Sons of Norway *Viking* wrote. The *Annals* of the American Academy of Political and Social Science stated: "Professor Bjork's story of Norwegian engineers in America is not only fascinating but instructive, because he succeeds so admirably in developing the technical backgrounds against which his subjects move and make their important contributions."

In *A Long Pull from Stavanger: The Reminiscences of a Norwegian Immigrant* (1945), by Birger Osland, the efficient long-time treasurer of the Association, the reader gains insight into the life and experiences of one who "made good" in America. A successful career may be viewed as a part of the Americanization process, but the book also gives more, as the *American Journal of Sociology* indicated when it stated that its value "lies in its portrayal of the social, cultural, and institutional developments of the Norwegian immigrants in Chicago." Another successful career mirrored in autobiographical format is Laurence M. Larson's *The Log Book of a Young Immigrant*, published posthumously in 1938. Larson told of his life and academic career as a respected student and professor of history in the University of Illinois, but also interpreted the immigrant experience.

Larson's *The Changing West and Other Essays*, which appeared in 1937, presents a mature scholar's view of a variety of topics, including "The Norwegian Element in the Field of American Scholarship," "Tellef Grundysen and the Beginnings of Norwegian-American Fiction," "Hjalmar Hjorth Boyesen," "The Lay Preacher in Pioneer Times," and others. The *Mississippi Valley Historical Review* had this to say of the essays: "Interpretive rather than factual, sympathetic rather than critical, this volume continues the high standard of other volumes of the publishers. The author himself, unmentioned in the text, was one of the finest products of Norwegian culture in America.''

Another important book treating the life of a well-known Norwegian American is *Laur. Larsen: Pioneer College President*, by his daughter, the late Professor Karen Larsen of St. Olaf College. The volume was published in 1936 with some support from alumni of Luther College, where Larsen served as first president and participated in many phases of immigrant religious and cultural life. Agnes M. Larson, long chairman of the department of history at St. Olaf, painted a revealing, sympathetic, and even flattering picture of an outstanding man of affairs in *John A. Johnson: An Uncommon American*. This seventeenth volume in the series was published in 1969.

The Special Publications series also includes translated works. *A Chronicle of Old Muskego: The Diary of Søren Bache, 1839–1847*, which appeared in 1951, was translated and edited by Clarence A. Clausen and Andreas Elviken. It is an important source of information for the early years in a settlement, a major ''mother colony.'' Bache played a leading role in the Muskego community; in his modest chronicle he imparted the flavor of life in southeastern Wisconsin during the pioneer period. Another insight into early conditions in Wisconsin and northeastern Iowa is provided by *The Diary of Elisabeth Koren, 1847–1872*, translated and edited by David T. Nelson and published in 1955. Mrs. Koren was a sensitive minister's wife who suffered in the harsh surroundings where her husband and she served. The *American Qonian* correctly appraised her writing: ''The diary is a highly personal record written by an observing and intelligent young bride with a keen appreciation of nature but with the poise and restraint that belonged to a cultured lady of the time.''

An account expressing a similar theme is *Grass of the Earth: Immigrant Life in Dakota Country*, published in 1950. It was written by Aagot Raaen ''in a simple style'' that ''has all the drama and suspense of a novel,'' in the words of the *Pacific Northwest Quarterly*. The *Wisconsin Magazine of History* welcomed the book as a ''contribution to the human documentation of the great American epic.'' The magazine concluded that ''readers who deplore the loss of many an untold odyssey of the frontier will be grateful to Miss Raaen.''

Also for the early period, we find a study of a subject that warrants several volumes. Professor Arlow William Andersen's *The Immigrant Takes His Stand: The Norwegian-American Press and Public Affairs, 1847–1872*, published in 1953, traces the development of a secular press and its political stance before and after the Civil War period. Its analysis of editorial positions "will prove useful to both students of Norwegian-American affairs and students of public opinion among the immigrants and of the Americanization process," according to the *American-Scandinavian Review*.

The eighteenth publication in the series and the fifty-fifth volume issued by the Association is *A Folk Epic: The Bygdelag in America*, by Dr. Odd S. Lovoll. As a sesquicentennial publication, it helps observe the arrival of the first boatload of Norwegian immigrants on the *Restauration* in 1825. It is the story of common folk who also knew the pangs of nostalgia for the homeland districts from which they had migrated.

XIV

THE AUTHORS SERIES

THE Association's editorial program from the start called for a biographical series, but studies of prominent individuals have generally fallen under other headings. A distinct Authors Series, however, was launched by Professor Bjork in 1963 with the publication of Dr. Clarence A. Glasrud's *Hjalmar Hjorth Boyesen*. Boyesen, who was able to enter the national American field of letters, never fully identified with his Norwegian background. He was thus in a sense an outsider so far as the immigrant community was concerned. His talent was also limited, but, as Professor Harald Næss indicates in *Scandinavian Studies*, "a felicitous use of words masked" this fact. He was, nevertheless, an interesting figure. Dr. Marc L. Ratner, in *American Literature*, complimented the author, who, he said, "has done remarkably well in arranging . . . scattered materials into a sympathetic and readable account."

The second volume in the series was published in 1966. One of the most colorful and controversial — as well as influential — men in the early Norwegian-American community was Rasmus Bjørn Anderson. He was at the center of most immigrant cultural activity and was perhaps the first educated Norwegian American of prominence. Professor Lloyd Hustvedt, under the title *Rasmus Bjørn Anderson: Pioneer Scholar*, presented his life and career in its many phases. Dr. Erik Wahlgren wrote of the book in *Scandinavian Studies*: "This work has developed into a broad, mature presentation of that 'teacher, translator, writer, diplomat, and editor etc. etc.' . . . This is a fascinating book and an important one.'' There have been numerous favorable reviews of the volume, which earned the McKnight Prize for the best biography produced by a Minnesotan in 1966.

The two books in the Authors Series have a total of 626 pages; they constitute a significant contribution to the Association's program — and to the field of immigration history. The series should be expanded by many studies of men and women who enriched Norwegian-American culture.

XV

TOPICAL STUDIES

THE Topical Studies series was introduced in 1971 to accommodate shorter volumes, especially doctoral dissertations, considered worthy of publication. Dr. Bjork, in introducing this fifth category of studies, remarked: "I am confident that contributions to it, short in length and long on interpretation, will add a refreshing dimension to our publications." The cover design of the first and only volume to date displays a knight in armor with drawn sword to indicate that the series will include interpretations that challenge traditional views.

The single book in Topical Studies is *A Voice of Protest*, by Dr. Jon Wefald — a volume of less than a hundred pages. Reviewers were pleased to have thus made available theses of this kind; usually they are "consigned to the bottom vaults of university libraries," as Dr. David Brye stated in a review for the *Journal of American History*. He joined some scholars in disagreeing with certain points of methodology, as well as with some conclusions Dr. Wefald made about Norwegian-American participation in progressive politics. Other reviews, however, were laudatory. In all, the study generated the debate and stimulated the objections that were anticipated.

The five series together consist of more than 13,550 carefully edited pages of great value — an impressive achievement for a fifty-year period. On occasion, works published elsewhere but within the Association's field of interest have been purchased and distributed to the members.

XVI

THE ASSOCIATION'S LEADERSHIP

THE success of the Norwegian-American Historical Association cannot be separated from the able and dedicated leadership it has enjoyed throughout its existence. While some of its officers and promoters have been discussed above, nevertheless it is necessary to introduce collectively the individuals who have functioned at the center of activity and have carried the major responsibility for sustaining the organization.

The executive board has consisted of the president, one or more vice presidents, the secretary, the treasurer, and an increasing number of members; twenty-five are allowed by the present by-laws. The managing editor has been an ex-officio member. The editorial board (now the board of publications) has conducted its affairs by correspondence. The executive board has met from time to time at the call of the president and at the triennial gatherings to deliberate and to act on the Association's business. The major officers now constitute an executive committee, which periodically conducts separate meetings.

All leaders have served without remuneration. Indeed, the accomplishments of the Association reflect a constant labor of love and donated services. The executive board has included men of means, high cultural interest, and strong ethnic pride. They have been quick to grasp the significance of the Association's work and have acted on their conviction. They have both contributed and solicited money and have held to a steady course through the years.

The visible results of their efforts, combined with those of scholars, have been published works, the gathering of historical documents, and financial security.

The Reverend D. G. Ristad was president for the first five years, after which time he served as vice president until his death in 1938 at the age of seventy-five. Ristad represented the best traditions of Norwegian-American life. He exhibited a unique ability to fathom the cultural wealth inherent in the immigrant community. He excelled as an educator and clergyman, was an active and dynamic force in the *bygdelag*, had strong literary and historical interests, and possessed a sensitive poetic talent. Pastor Ristad was in complete accord with the aims of the Association, and he contributed substantially to its rapid acceptance among Norwegian Americans. He worked closely with the other leaders to establish a sound program in the early years.

Ristad was succeeded as president by Magnus Swenson. Swenson served until 1936, when poor health made it impossible for him to accept re-election. The second president, who resided in Madison, Wisconsin, had behind him a successful engineering and business career. He also revealed a vital interest in education and in Norwegian-American affairs — qualities that made him eminently suited for the position of leadership to which the Association had called him. His successor, Arthur Andersen, was also a man of business, who had founded an internationally known accounting firm in Chicago that bears his name. He supported the Association with generous contributions and energetic leadership from 1926 to 1942, making possible the granting of fellowships in aid of research and writing. He served as vice president for three additional years.

At the sixth triennial meeting in 1942, the Association found its next president in the person of Olaf Halvorson of Huntington Park, California. After a career as a high-school teacher, he became prosperous when oil was discovered on his property and as a result of subsequent real-estate investments. He fathered and generously supported the project that resulted in *West of the Great Divide*.

S. J. Arnesen, then publisher of *Nordisk Tidende* (Nordic Times) in Brooklyn, became president in 1951, after Halvorson's retirement. He promoted the Association effectively in the New York area. In 1954, Arnesen was succeeded by J. A. Aasgaard, retired president of the Evangelical Lutheran Church, whose warm personality and enthusiasm inspired the Association for two trienniums.

Lionel George Thorsness, who had been vice president since 1945, held the presidency for nine years, from 1960 to 1969. He was a well-known lawyer in Chicago who gave valuable leadership. Magnus Bjorndal succeeded him in 1969, after serving as vice president from 1960. He grappled with the task of building the Theodore C. Blegen Fellowship Fund, and, at the time of his death in 1971, was engaged in a program to enlist greater financial support for the Association in the East. Bjorndal was one of the men in the "migration of skills" described in *A Saga in Steel and Concrete*. An engineer by training, in 1935 he founded the Tech Laboratories, which produce complicated electrical equipment in Jersey City.

Dr. Gunnar Gundersen, prominent physician in La Crosse, Wisconsin, and a member of the executive board, filled out Bjorndal's term as president to 1972. At the triennial meeting in Minneapolis that year, Dr. Kenneth O. Bjork accepted the position — a new practice in the Association, as he would serve in the double capacity of president and editor.

For periods of time, the Association has had more than one functioning vice president. Laurence M. Larson was the first person to occupy this position, later contributing substantially to the work of the editorial board. L. W. Boe, president of St. Olaf College and an enthusiastic supporter of the Association, who on many occasions expressed strong faith in its potential, was vice president from 1939 to his death in 1942. After World War II, Axel Waerenskjold, Søren Røinestad, Marthinius A. Strand, David T. Nelson, and Andrew A. Wigeland, long-time treasurer of the Association, all occupied the position. The incumbent vice president, Mr. Roy N. Thorshov, a Minneapolis architect and active promoter of community projects and Norwegian cultural endeavors, was elected in 1972.

A number of qualified men with keen knowledge of financial operations have been in charge of the Association's treasury. O. M. Oleson, a successful businessman in Dodge City, Iowa, was appointed treasurer in 1925, with J. Jørgen Thompson as financial secretary. Oleson had accepted the responsibility on the condition that Birger Osland occupy a position of assistant treasurer. Osland replaced Oleson in 1930 and served until his resignation in 1951.

His faithful custodianship of finances has been treated elsewhere.

From 1951 to 1969, Andrew A. Wigeland — like Osland a Chicago businessman — continued the highly professional service of his predecessors as treasurer. "He kept a firm hand on the financial rudder," as his obituary in a *Newsletter* of 1970 states, "and helped guide the organization through two decades of rising prices and considerable uncertainty regarding the future." His interest encompassed all aspects of the Association's work, from membership rolls to editorial undertakings.

Two other Chicago men have served as treasurers. From 1969 to 1972, Norman O. Olson gave vital direction to financial activities, and, since 1972, Mr. Leonard W. Arentsen has been able custodian of the Association's resources. Despite recent uncertainty and falling returns on investments, the organization is in excellent financial condition.

Erik Hetle and David T. Nelson also served as financial secretaries before 1939, when this office merged with that of the secretary. The secretary has been at the center of activity in housekeeping, answering inquiries, promoting membership, raising money, preparing triennial meetings, setting up reports, and also, for most of the time, in serving as archivist. Only three individuals have occupied this position, all of them professors at St. Olaf College: O. E. Rølvaag, J. Jørgen Thompson, and Lloyd Hustvedt.

A number of men, as members of the executive board, have made significant contributions to the Association, but space limitations prevent an adequate description of them.Typical has been the work of Judge Derwood Johnson of Waco, Texas, who drafted the present constitution and by-laws of the Association; of Mr. Henning C. Boe, editor of *Western Viking*, who has stimulated interest in our work in the Pacific Northwest; and of the late Dr. Richard W. Giere of Minneapolis, whose efforts and visions embraced both membership and realistic financial support.

The board of publications has been discussed in a previous chapter. It now consists of the following individuals: Kenneth O. Bjork, editor, Arlow W. Andersen, Clarence A. Clausen, Erik J. Friis, Clarence A. Glasrud, Einar Haugen, Odd S. Lovoll, Peter A. Munch, and Carlton C. Qualey.

XVII

APPRAISALS

THE Association has done its work without fanfare and social activity; festivals have had almost no place in its program. But the triennial meetings, seventeen in all — counting the 1975 one — have generally featured a festive banquet. All but two of them have been held in Minneapolis. On Monday, October 7, 1935, the Association also celebrated its tenth anniversary at St. Olaf, although in no elaborate manner. The college conferred honorary doctoral degrees on Theodore C. Blegen, D. G. Ristad, and Birger Osland on this occasion.

Festivity also characterized the silver jubilee in 1950. Senator Edward J. Thye of Minnesota chaired the sponsoring committee, and on Friday, October 6, more than 250 friends and members assembled at St. Olaf College for the twenty-fifth anniversary celebration — on the very day of the founding. Several addresses, reminiscences, and short talks by guest speakers and by individuals active in the organization's affairs were presented at different sessions. Professor Franklin D. Scott of Northwestern University concluded his featured address by hailing the Association as ''a prototype for other groups who would search the past to gain understanding of themselves, and of the America they have helped to build.''

At the tenth triennial meeting in 1954 the American Association for State and Local History presented a certificate of merit — result-

ing from an action it had taken in 1951 — to the Norwegian-
American Historical Association for "celebrating in a most appropriate manner its 25th anniversary; for publishing three outstanding
contributions to the field of state and local history . . . for publishing the best single history of a nationality group . . . and for
achieving an enviable reputation by continuous publication for over
a quarter century."

Walter Muir Whitehill, in his prodigious study, *Independent Historical Societies: An Enquiry into Their Research and Publication
Functions and Their Financial Future*, published in 1962, included
a statement about the Association. In a flattering account of its
history, he commented on the publication program by stating: "Ad-
miration for the variety of subject, the quality of research, editing,
and book production involved in this remarkable series can only be
exceeded by amazement that so much has been accomplished with
such limited financial resources."

Professor Rudolph J. Vecoli, professor of history and director of
the Immigration Research Center at the University of Minnesota,
sums up the general view of the Association's work in an evaluation
solicited for the present publication. It reads:

"This history of the Norwegian-American Historical Association reminds us that there is nothing new under the sun, not even
ethnic studies. While the discovery of ethnicity was being an-
nounced with great fanfare, the NAHA was quietly approaching its
fiftieth anniversary. Five decades of dedicated, intelligent work
have created an extensive library of publications and a rich archives
of records on the Norwegian experience in America. Thanks to the
NAHA, the history of the Norwegians has been more fully
documented than that of any other immigrant group in America.
Blessed with the leadership of such outstanding historians as
Theordore C. Blegen and Kenneth O. Bjork, the NAHA has consistently maintained the highest standards in its research and publication programs. Unfortunately, few other ethnic historical
societies have approached it in quality of scholarship and diligence
of effort. If they had, our task today in writing a pluralistic history
of America would be much easier. But for those of us who came
after, the NAHA served as an inspiration and model. It is well to
remember that for half a century, without federal funds or founda-

tion grants, the Norwegian-American community has supported the Association's efforts to preserve and publish its history. As we lobby for appropriations under the Ethnic Heritage Act, we should never forget that the primary responsibility for the preservation of an ethnic heritage rests with the ethnic group itself. Unless it believes in and is willing to work for the preservation of that heritage, no amount of federal funding will keep it alive. Perhaps that is the most important lesson we can learn from the history of the NAHA.''

XVIII

A PLAN FOR THE FUTURE

IN recent years, we in the Association have often discussed the desirability of encouraging studies in a variety of fields. Some have been undertaken and the results published; more have remained in the planning stage. We should like to mention a few of the projects which, though frequently mentioned, still await the interested scholar.

Years ago, Dr. Bjork proposed to Theodore C. Blegen, then editor of the Association, that we must undertake an intensive study of a typical Norwegian settlement in the Upper Middle West. Such a project would include the migration story itself — its origins, the crossing, travel inland, pioneer experience — and would bring the account down to the present. It would explore all phases of life — social, economic, religious, political, and cultural — and would give painstaking attention to all currents of American and immigrant influence. If done with care, patience, and mature judgment, it could be a distinguished contribution to national history. Closely related projects would be an imaginative record of a single farm, both as a separate unit and in its relationship to a village or small town, and a study of immigrant farm life with stress on the economic and social factors.

If we have given inadequate attention to the rural community, our neglect of the city has been even greater. Where are the students of urban life, trained in sociology as well as history, who could give comprehensive treatment to the Norwegians in such vital centers as Minneapolis, Chicago, Greater New York, San Francisco, and Seattle?

One of the larger projects we have often spoken of is the preparation of a series of volumes of translated "America letters," both those written to kinsmen and friends in Europe and those sent to the editors of the Norwegian-language press from various settlements in the New World. If thoughtfully planned and executed, such an undertaking could add immeasurably to an understanding of grassroots American life and provide scholars with material for countless studies in specialized fields.

There is need for a number of volumes on the academies, schools, and colleges founded and supported by immigrants and their descendants. The part played by the academies in particular cries for interpretation by a sympathetic and versatile scholar, but equally significant would be a study of the colleges as a whole — one that relates them thoughtfully to all the forces at work in new-world life. The culture of America, its influence on the immigrant and his contribution to it, cannot be separated from the story of educational institutions.

The Association has published some biographies, but many more are required if the Norwegian-American role in such fields as business, the professions, and politics is to be fully understood. These must be of a scholarly nature — not merely eulogies of successful men. Similarly, we need broad monographic studies of immigrant doctors, businessmen, lawyers, and officials in state and federal government. Closely related to biography is autobiography. Every effort should be made to encourage selected persons to write of their experiences.

We have recently published a full-length interpretation of the *bygdelag* movement in North America under the title *A Folk Epic*. This scholarly work by Dr. Lovoll reminds us of other organizations — social, literary, and musical — that flourished and in some instances still flourish in the Norwegian-American community. Special attention should be given to those organizations that made contributions in the realm of singing and dramatic performance.

Despite much talk about the role of the immigrant and his children in the area of politics, we have published only one slim volume, *A Voice of Protest*, that comes to grips with the subject. Although Jon Wefald has pioneered this field, a great deal remains to be done with the role of the common folk — their voting habits, shifts in party affiliation, and retention of communitarian concepts in opposition to a prevailing emphasis on individualism. We would welcome studies of various aspects of this fascinating subject — of forces and movements, of issues and events — and even more a comprehensive survey of political activity from frontier days to the present. No effort should be spared in utilizing the new techniques of quantification.

And what of the Norwegian-language press? Although many students have drawn upon this invaluable source, no one — with the single exception of Professor Arlow W. Andersen in his *The Immigrant Takes His Stand* — has undertaken a serious study of the role played by the newspapers over the past hundred years. There is material in this treasure-trove for many investigations — depending on the interests of the researchers — and any approach will yield sources for numerous additional publications dealing with Norwegian-American life.

Thus far we have done very little with the subject of sports, especially those "dependent on snow and ice and ski and skate," but also those involving team competition on turf and cinder track. We have not remembered the athletic and rifle clubs, the mutual-aid and insurance companies. Nor have we met our obligations with respect to selected diaries; some are at hand, others are yet to be found. Despite frequent accounts of church activity, we have yet to analyze the many forces — in Europe and America — that have shaped this immigrant institution, led to controversy and division, union and present form of organization. Discussions of the subject of "Americanization" have focused on language, but the congregation of today was already largely formed while Norwegian was still the language of the pulpit. To make matters worse, the part played by Methodists, Baptists, Unitarians, liberals, Mormons, and others in immigrant religious life has been treated only superficially.

Similarly, the stories of the Norwegians in Canada, the southern and western states, Alaska, and especially the Great Plains have still to be told. Until this has been done in a manner that tests the skill and patience of the dedicated scholar, we must confess that our work has only begun. We must also translate and publish more documentary material — the records of organizations and individuals, the papers of leaders in a variety of enterprises, vital narratives, lists of manuscripts, guides to sources, an index for our *Norwegian-American Studies*, and the like.

In recent years we have created two new categories of publications — an Authors Series and Topical Studies. The purpose of the first is self-evident, and two biographies of writers have appeared in print. The mere existence of this series should encourage more books of equal merit. We hope to publish Professor Nina Draxten's excellent biography of Kristofer Janson in America some time early in 1976, and Professor Henriette C. K. Naeseth's translations of Marcus Thrane's American-based plays — together with a probing analysis of his career in the New World — should be ready for the press soon thereafter. We anticipate manuscripts dealing with such writers as Waldemar Ager, Simon Johnson, Julius Baumann, and many others. A special place on this shelf of books is reserved for a fresh volume on O. E. Rølvaag, who served as the Association's first secretary.

Topical Studies was launched as an open invitation to young scholars — usually products of our graduate schools — to submit, in condensed form, the results of their researches in areas of vital interest to the Association. In 1935, our first president, D. G. Ristad, summed up the first decade of the Association's work with these words: "The future belongs to our youth, especially to intellectually cultured youth; the inheritance is theirs; they shall make it grow. The Norwegian-American Historical Association looks to them to carry on the work, suppport it, and make it count in the larger life of the American people." We do indeed need more scholars to take up the host of tasks that confront us. It is our sincere hope that graduate and post-doctoral students, their dissertations completed, will consider revising and submitting their manuscripts with a view to their inclusion in our Topical Studies. Dr. Wefald's *A Voice of Protest*, mentioned above, set a fine standard of competence and struck the right note of controversy to give the series an even greater vitality and interest than was hoped for at its inception.

If youth is to be served, so too are the mature scholars in a variety of fields, who must co-operate with historians in the future. We have in mind sociologists and psychologists, whose skills and knowledge are essential in fully grasping the subtle processes of accommodation and assimilation, the problems of the second, third, and later generations of Americans — indeed of providing an acceptable definition of Americanism itself. In this day of renewed interest in ethnicity, we are equally concerned with the theme of conservation, the retention of values and cultural characteristics in living generations. We need help from geographers, whose investigations increasingly focus on the human factor, and also from demographers. We must encourage physicians and health officials to study the problems of sanitation and disease among immigrants and their children. We can use the skills of agronomists and students of ecology, of home economists, of musicians and actors, of literary historians and critics, of philosophers and theologians. Even more, we need the co-operation of creative writers and artists who will sense the richness of the immigration story and, like Rølvaag and Moberg, will record for posterity the essence of various aspects of that great human experience. The current popularity of such films as *The Emigrants* and *The New Land* is testimony to a keen public interest.

If full benefit is to be derived from the work already completed and from studies to be made in the future, it is necessary to prepare pamphlets and books, written in popular style and attractively printed, for use in the schools and by adults who are disinclined to read the publications of scholars. We are thinking in particular of the opportunity awaiting persons with a talent for writing children's stories. What a wealth of material awaits them·in the 55 publications already distributed by the Association!

Some well-meaning persons have asked if we would not now be justified in winding up the work of the Norwegian-American Historical Association and closing shop after a half-century of effort. Such an attitude obviously strikes us as absurd. We are only well launched on our task. But it is true that what has been possible in the period from 1925 to 1975 will be more difficult in the future. The services of the editor and secretary, for example, have been voluntary; both have had other full-time positions requiring the major portions of their energy and working hours. The attendant loss to the Association is incalculable when one considers lost opportunities both for research and in the collection and processing of documentary materials. We hope before long to secure adequate funds for an endowed chair of immigration history and a salaried director. These goals cannot be attained too soon. The Association appreciates the announcement by President Sidney A. Rand of St. Olaf's intention, if adequate funds are raised in the college's centennial appeal, to allocate a substantial sum for the creation of a chair in immigration history.

When one reflects on what remains to be done, one recalls the dedicated services of men and women no longer with us: Rølvaag, Laurence M. Larson, Ristad, Kristian Prestgard, Marcus Lee Hansen, Knut Gjerset, Martin B. Ruud, Arthur Andersen, Birger Osland, David T. Nelson, Karen Larsen, J. Jørgen Thompson, Magnus Swenson, Agnes M. Larson, Andrew E. Wigeland, Lionel G. Thorsness, Magnus Bjorndal, Richard W. Giere, and others. We reserve special mention for the late Theodore C. Blegen, managing editor to 1960 and inspiring mentor to all of us. It is significant that at every crucial stage of our history the executive board has met the crisis with a frontal attack. We recall in particular the words once addressed by Osland, long-time treasurer, to Dr. Blegen: "When the need is there, the money will be forthcoming." And it has been — a remarkable tribute to the contributions of individuals deeply convinced of the value of historical research.

The Association can do a distinguished service to American history in the next half-century only if it has the needed talent, courage, imagination, leadership, and financial resources. Those who give of their means contribute as much as those who write and edit books or perform secretarial and archival services. One thing is certain: there is no room in the organization for smallness of thinking, jealousy, lack of vision. In a literal sense, the thing we are doing and hope to continue doing is bigger than ourselves and requires the co-operation of all. This means the joint effort of old and young, scholars and businessmen, officers and members — all who are willing to forward a cause whose benefits will survive those who now carry the major responsibility for it.

APPENDIX

THE OFFICERS OF THE ASSOCIATION

PRESIDENTS

D. G. Ristad	1925–30
Magnus Swenson	1930–36
Arthur Andersen	1936–42
Olaf Halvorson	1942–51
S. J. Arnesen	1951–54
J. A. Aasgaard	1954–60
Lionel G. Thorsness	1960–69
Magnus Bjorndal	1969–71
Gunnar Gundersen	1971–72
*Kenneth O. Bjork	1972–

VICE PRESIDENTS

Laurence M. Larson
D. G. Ristad
L. W. Boe
Arthur Andersen
Axel Waerenskjold
Lionel G. Thorsness
Søren Røinestad
Marthinius A. Strand
David T. Nelson
Magnus Bjorndal
Andrew A. Wigeland
*Roy N. Thorshov

SECRETARIES

O. E. Rølvaag	1925–31
J. Jørgen Thompson	1931–59
*Lloyd Hustvedt	1959–

TREASURERS

O. M. Oleson	1925–30
Birger Osland	1930–51
Andrew A. Wigeland	1951–69
Norman O. Olson	1969–72
*Leonard W. Arentsen	1972–

FINANCIAL SECRETARIES

J. Jørgen Thompson
Erik Hetle
David T. Nelson

In 1939 this office merged with the secretary's.

*Denotes incumbent officers. Officers not currently serving are listed in order of election.

BOARD OF PUBLICATIONS

Theodore C. Blegen, Ed.1925–60
*Kenneth O. Bjork, Ed. 1960–
Knut Gjerset
Kristian Prestgard
Laurence M. Larson
Paul Knaplund
Marcus L. Hansen
Brynjolf J. Hovde
Martin B. Ruud
Carl L. Lokke

*Arlow W. Andersen
*Clarence A. Clausen
*Erik J. Friis
*Clarence A. Glasrud
*Einar Haugen
*Odd S. Lovoll
*Peter A. Munch
*Carlton C. Qualey

EXECUTIVE BOARD MEMBERS

A. C. Floan
Knut Gjerset
E. G. Kvamme
Fredric Schaefer
S. J. Arnesen
O. M. Oleson
J. A. Holmboe
A. N. Rygg
David T. Nelson
Olaf Halvorson
Arthur Andersen
L. W. Boe
Magnus Bjorndal
Mrs. Inga Frodesen
Sverre Arestad
Gunnar E. Gunderson
Lionel G. Thorsness
Norman O. Olson
Andrew E. Wigeland

Sevrin A. Haram
Roy N. Thorshov
Truman Eddy
Richard W. Giere
*Oscar A. Anderson
*Henning C. Boe
*John Christianson
*Arthur O. Davidson
*Reidar Dittmann
*Gunnar Gundersen
*J. Bernard Jacobsen
*Derwood Johnson
*Andrew A. Kindem
*Norma Arnesen Knutson
*Ole G. Landsverk
*Rolf A. Syrdal
*Norman Wigeland
*Harry J. Williams

REGIONAL CHAIRMEN

A. N. Rygg
Gunnar Lund
Christian Brant
Hans Ustrud
John Brown
M. E. Moe
Mrs. Oakley Kissam Brown
C. Martin Alsager

H. G. Thorpe
G. T. Lee
John Nornborg
Frida Bue-Homnes
E. Nyman Figved
S. J. Arnesen
Julius E. Olson
G. T. Lee

Herman C. Nordlie
Axel Arneson
B. L. Wick
Christian Olsen
J. A. Quam
Alice R. Sonsteby
A. T. Strandness
R. A. Nestos
R. O. Richards
George H. Gutru
Peter Berge
Hjalmar Rued Holand
Olaf Halvorson
John Heitman
Olaf Hove
Andreas Helland
Peter Norbeck
G. M. Bruce
N. A. Grevstad
Mrs. Sigrid Hakstad

Arthur Andersen
Helmer Blegen
Kristine Haugen
O. I. Hertsgaard
J. M. Johnson
Charles E. Larsen
George Tweed
Gustav G. Martin
Carl Søyland
Arne Williamson
Peter Myrvald
Magnus Bjorndal
Carl E. Abrahamson
Mrs. Jon Norstog
Carl E. Moe
Russel Johnson
Harry J. Williams
Arne Bjorndal
Arne Tvete